SOVIET FOREIGN POLICY, 1930–33

STUDIES IN SOVIET HISTORY AND SOCIETY
General Editor: R. W. Davies

The series consists of works by members or associates of the inter-disciplinary Centre for Russian and East European Studies of the University of Birmingham, England. Special interests of the Centre include Soviet economic and social history, contemporary Soviet economics and planning, science and technology, sociology and education.

John Barber
SOVIET HISTORIANS IN CRISIS, 1928–1932

Philip Hanson
TRADE AND TECHNOLOGY IN SOVIET–WESTERN RELATIONS

Jonathan Haslam
SOVIET FOREIGN POLICY, 1930–33

Nicholas Lampert
THE TECHNICAL INTELLIGENTSIA AND THE SOVIET STATE

Robert Lewis
SCIENCE AND INDUSTRIALISATION IN THE USSR

Neil Malcolm
SOVIET POLITICAL SCIENTISTS AND AMERICAN POLITICS

David Mandel
THE PETROGRAD WORKERS AND THE FALL OF THE OLD REGIME

THE PETROGRAD WORKERS AND THE SOVIET SEIZURE OF POWER

Roger Skurski
SOVIET MARKETING AND ECONOMIC DEVELOPMENT

J. N. Westwood
SOVIET LOCOMOTIVE TECHNOLOGY DURING INDUSTRIAL-
ISATION, 1928–1952

SOVIET FOREIGN POLICY, 1930-33

The Impact of the Depression

Jonathan Haslam
Lecturer in Soviet Diplomatic History
University of Birmingham

St. Martin's Press   New York

All rights reserved. For information, write:
St. Martin's Press, Inc., 175 Fifth Avenue, New York, NY 10010
Printed in Hong Kong
First published in the United States of America in 1983

ISBN 0-312-74838-8

Library of Congress Cataloging in Publication Data

Haslam, Jonathan.
  Soviet foreign policy, 1930-33.

  Bibliography: p.
  Includes index.
  1. Soviet Union—Foreign relations—1917-1945.
I. Title.
DK267.H3354 1983   327.47   82-22996
ISBN 0-312-74838-8

In memory of E. A. H.

Contents

Preface

This is envisaged as the first of four volumes in a history of Soviet foreign policy from the onset of the Great Depression until the Great Patriotic War, covering the period 1930 to 1941.

As the reader will note, there is no serious attempt to cover the history of the Comintern during these years. Its activities have only been touched upon where they appear to answer the tactical needs of Soviet diplomacy. This cavalier treatment should not be taken to mean that the Comintern had no *raison d'être* of its own. It is because the late E.H. Carr has completed a history of the organisation during this period and there was no sense in trying to duplicate his efforts. It will also be apparent that there are certain countries whose relations with the USSR receive scant treatment, but my priority has been to highlight the most important events which inevitably has cast some states into the shadows.

Wherever possible primary sources have been used. These include documents selected and published from the archives of the Soviet Foreign Ministry. Unfortunately western scholars are still denied direct access to the archives themselves. This has necessitated extensive use of the contemporary Soviet press and consultation of material in British, French, German and Italian archives, to provide a more comprehensive understanding of events.

Obtaining access to these and other sources required the help of many individuals and institutions. A considerable debt of gratitude is therefore owed to the following: the British Academy, the Italian Cultural Institute and Birmingham University (including its Centre for Russian and East European Studies) for the funds which facilitated research both here and abroad; to Dr Benedikz (Birmingham University Library); Jenny Brine (librarian at CREES); Angela Raspin (British Library of Political and Economic Sciences); the staffs of the British Library; the Bibliothèque de Documentation International Contemporaine (Nanterre); Cambridge University Library; the Marx Memorial

Library; the Institute of the History of the USSR Library in the
Soviet Academy of Sciences (Moscow); the Lenin Library
(Moscow); the Central State Archive (Rome); the Italian Foreign
Ministry Archive; the French Foreign Ministry Archive; the
French National Archives (Overseas Section); the Public Record
Office at Kew; to Mr Reid of the Imperial War Museum and the
late Mr Hiscock of Foreign and Commonwealth Office Library
and Records, for access to books and documents in their care; to
Renate Barany and Janet Evans for checking my German trans-
lations; to Francesco Benvenuti (Bologna University), Judith
Bloomfield, Professor Ian Nish (LSE), and Mr Arfon Rees (Keele
University) for their help in obtaining material; to Dr Taki Hara
for the translation of Japanese memoirs; to Dr Julian Cooper for
his criticisms, and to others at the Soviet Industrialisation Project
Seminar at CREES in Birmingham for the often unseen but none
the less vital influence they have exerted on the progress of my
work; to Professor J.A.S. Grenville (Birmingham University) for
kindly reading the penultimate draft and suggesting helpful
amendments; and, last but not least, a special mention is
required for the late E.H. Carr, and also Professor R.W. Davies,
for their ready guidance, generous attention and constant
encouragement, without which the book would have been much
the poorer, though this in no way diminishes my responsibility for
any flaws in the work as a whole.

Birmingham University   JONATHAN HASLAM

Abbreviations and Acronyms

AA	*Auswärtiges Amt (German Foreign Ministry)*
AD	*Archives Diplomatiques* (Diplomatic Archives)
Amtorg	Amerikano-Russkaya Torgovaya Palata (Russo-American Chamber of Commerce)
AN	*Archives Nationales* (National Archives)
ASD	*Archivio Storico Diplomatico* (Diplomatic History Archives)
CAB	*Cabinet Minutes*
CCP	Chinese Communist Party
CER	Chinese Eastern Railway
CFAID	Comité Franco-Allemand d' Information et Documentation (Franco-German Committee of Information and Documentation)
Comintern	Kommunisticheskii Internatsional (Communist International)
Cong Sang/ Cong San Dang	Indochinese Communist Party
DBFP	*Documents on British Foreign Policy*
DDF	*Documents Diplomatiques Français* (French Diplomatic Documents)
DDI	*Documenti Diplomatici Italiani* (Italian Diplomatic Documents)
DVP SSR	*Dokumenty Vneshnei Politiki SSSR* (Foreign Policy Documents of the USSR)
FO	*Foreign Office*
IMTFE	*International Military Tribunal Far East*
IVMV	*Istoriya Vtoroi Mirovoi Voiny* (History of the Second World War)
JCP	Japanese Communist Party
KPD	Kommunistische Partei Deutschlands (German Communist Party)

Narkomindel	Narodnyi Komissariat Inostrannykh Del (People's Commissariat of Foreign Affairs)
Narkomvneshtorg	Narodnyi Komissariat Vneshnei Torgovly (People's Commissariat of Foreign Trade)
NC	Neville Chamberlain
NSDAP	National Sozialistische Deutsche Arbeiter Partei (National Socialist German Workers' Party)
OGPU	Ob"edinennoe Gosudarstvennoe Politicheskoe Upravlenie (Unified State Political Administration − political police)
PCF	Parti Communiste Français
Politburo	Political Bureau of the Soviet Communist Party Central Committee
Polpred	Polnomochnyi Predstavitel' (Plenipotentiary)
PV SSSR	Pogranichnye Voiska SSSR (Border Forces of the USSR)
Rabkrin	Narodnyi Komissariat Raboche-Krest'yanskoi Inspektsii (People's Commissariat of Workers' and Peasants' Inspection)
Revvoensovet	Revolyutsionnyi Voennyi Sovet (Revolutionary Military Council)
RSDLP	Russian Social Democratic Labour Party
RSFSR	Rossiiskaya Sovetskaya Federativnaya Sotsialisticheskaya Respublika (Russian Soviet Federative Socialist Republic)
Sovnarkom	Sovet Narodnykh Komissarov (Council of People's Commissars)
SPD	Sozial-Demokratische Partei Deutschlands (German Social Democratic Party)
TASS	Telegrafnoe Agentstvo Sovetskogo Soyuza (Telegraphic Agency of the Soviet Union)
Vesenkha	Vysshii Sovet Narodnogo Khozyaistva SSSR (Supreme Council of National Economy of the USSR)

1 The Bases of Foreign Policy under Stalin

The global economic depression unleashed by the collapse of prices on the Wall Street stock exchange in October 1929 had a momentous impact on relations between the Powers. The direct result was a wave of protectionism which swept the capitalist and semi-colonial world as each economy scrambled to secure markets from its rivals. This, complicated in Europe by Germany's inability to pay reparations to the victorious Powers of World War I, exacerbated existing political differences to an alarming degree. The indirect effects of the Depression were no less disturbing. The slump in world trade destroyed the livelihood of vast numbers of people; the resulting mass unemployment then provided fertile ground for extremist political agitation from both Right and Left.

The West was thus in disarray, both domestically and internationally, from 1930 to 1933, and this undoubtedly gave the Soviet Union much needed breathing-space for its domestic economic revolution. But it would be wrong to see the Russians snugly sheltered from the storm raging outside. On the contrary, peering nervously from their window they were only too conscious of the fact that by raising international tension to new heights, the Depression had increased the likelihood of a new war. And whereas they were content to see the West divided, they also saw a real danger that war would soon envelop themselves along with their potential adversaries. Indeed, it was in a desperate attempt to insulate fortress Russia from such a threat that the Soviet leadership had embarked on a five-year plan of industrial construction in 1929.

The five-year plan was rooted in Stalin's conception of the country's needs, his overriding aim being to make it impregnable to assault from abroad. With the plan already well advanced in February 1931, he gave this vivid rendition of his views:

1

It is sometimes asked whether it is not possible to slow down the tempo somewhat, to put a check on the movement. No, comrades, it is not possible! The tempo must not be reduced! ... To slacken the tempo would mean falling behind. And those who fall behind get beaten. But we do not want to be beaten. One feature of the history of old Russia was the continual beatings she suffered because of her backwardness. She was beaten by the Turkish beys. She was beaten by the Swedish feudal lords. She was beaten by the Polish and Lithuanian gentry. She was beaten by the British and French capitalists. She was beaten by the Japanese barons. All beat her – because of her backwardness, because of her military backwardness, cultural backwardness, agricultural backwardness. They beat her because to do so was profitable and could be done with impunity. You remember the words of the pre-revolutionary poet: "You are poor and abundant, mighty and impotent, Mother Russia". Those gentlemen were quite familiar with the verses of the old poet. They beat her, saying: "You are abundant", so one can enrich oneself at your expense. They beat her, saying: "You are poor and impotent", so you can be beaten and plundered with impunity. Such is the law of the exploiters – to beat the backward and the weak. It is the jungle law of capitalism. You are backward, you are weak – therefore you are wrong; hence you can be beaten and enslaved. You are mighty – therefore you are right; hence we must be wary of you.

That is why we must no longer lag behind.[1]

The promise was that the plan would, in the long term, so strengthen Soviet power that the rest of the world would be obliged to leave the USSR in peace. In the meantime, however, Soviet diplomats and the Comintern had to do their utmost, by one means or another, to win the country sufficient time to realise the plan.

The Soviet leadership never supposed that the world would simply stand still and watch whilst the citadel of revolution reinforced its ramparts. On the contrary, it had long been an article of faith that the stronger the Soviet Union became, the greater would be the animosity of international capitalism. The period of peaceful co-existence afforded Soviet power during the 1920s was attributed not merely to the reluctance of the West to launch an offensive. Soviet leaders also thought that their adversaries were less hostile because they misinterpreted the new economic policy as a return to capitalism. It thus seemed logical to suppose that its abandonment would lead to an aggressive response from the capitalist world. It is easy in retrospect to dismiss the recurring war scares in Moscow as mere "propaganda". But it must be remembered that Soviet leaders had their formative experience in relations with the West during the Allied war of intervention from 1918 to 1919. The crisis in Anglo-Soviet relations, ending in diplomatic rupture during the spring of 1927, only served to reinforce these anxieties, despite the fact that nothing more drastic occurred. For the lesson drawn from this experience was not that London never had any intention of taking serious action against Moscow, but that circumstances had forced the British to drop their plans. Asked whether the Soviet Government genuinely believed in the threat of Western intervention in August 1930, the head of the press and information department at the Commissariat of Foreign Affairs (Narkomindel) is reported to have said that:

the danger was a serious one and ... Soviet apprehensions were not so ridiculous as we seemed to think. He did not mean to say that foreign Governments were deliberately organising a military offensive against the Soviet Union which was one day to be launched. The Soviet press, no doubt, expressed itself in these terms, but the reason was that in explaining affairs to the masses extreme simplification was necessary. The menace was not so simple as that, but it was just as real. ... No one would deny that public opinion abroad was generally hostile to the Soviet Government, nor that in some countries there were powerful elements whose hostility was intense and implacable. This state of tension was being exploited by certain groups in several countries in the hope that it might reach such a pitch that, he might almost say, the guns would go off by themselves. By a policy of persistent provocation these groups hoped to force the hands of the Governments and leave them no alternative but recourse to arms. This was the meaning of the successive outrages upon Soviet representatives abroad, such, for example, as the shooting of the Soviet representative in Poland, or in the recent attempt upon the Soviet Legation in Warsaw. This was the meaning also of the Arcos raid, of Chang

Tso-lin's raid, of Chinese encroachment upon Russian rights in Manchuria, and of the spurious excitement aroused in France over the disappearance of General Kutepov. The Soviet Government, he said, had good reason to be apprehensive.[3]

These exaggerated fears placed a heavy burden on the USSR's inadequate defences. What is more, the burden grew as it became increasingly obvious that the short-term effects of implementing the five-year plan were to increase instead of lessening the country's vulnerability to attack. This was especially true with respect to the forced collectivisation of agriculture. The Red Army was called in to suppress revolts by disaffected peasants. Since the ranks were largely recruited from the better-fed sons of these rebels, the Red Army's role in the repression gravely weakened morale and drew its attention from the primary task of ensuring adequate national defence.[4] This, together with the concentration of the state's resources on the growth of industry, meant that the main task of Soviet diplomacy was "to guarantee peaceful conditions and freedom from external disturbance" for socialist construction. "The more significant our plans for construction, the faster the rates of growth, the greater is our concern to preserve peace", stressed Litvinov in an interview marking his appointment as Commissar for Foreign Affairs in July 1930.[5]

The implementation of the five-year plan also disrupted relations with the West. In order to pay for the necessary capital equipment it was buying from the advanced industrialised countries, the Soviets had to export ever greater quantities of the only items they produced in any abundance – raw materials, including grain. This is the point at which the five-year plan and the Great Depression coincided to create a major problem for the Soviet regime. The Wall Street crash further accelerated the falling price of wheat on the world market. On top of this dropped a mountain of Soviet grain. Since the revolution Russia had ceased to be the major exporter of grain that she had been. But now, requisitioning it from the peasants for export, the Bolsheviks boldly sought to resume Russia's former position in the world's grain markets under the most adverse conditions. The fatalism with which they considered the issue was typified in Varga's bland comment, writing as the head of the Soviet Institute of World Economy and World Politics in the late summer of 1929:

The appearance of the USSR once more in the world market as a grain exporter will inevitably lead to an increase in the supply of grain and, consequently, to a fall in price and to a new agrarian crisis.[6]

Such a prospect may have left Varga unmoved, but its political consequences were not long in making themselves felt and came to constitute one of the most intractable problems which bedevilled the work of the Narkomindel during the ensuing months. It affected relations with almost every country. Those states which depended heavily on the export of raw materials, particularly in Scandinavia and the Baltic, succumbed to fierce anti-Soviet agitation not merely from capitalists and farmers who suffered, but also from those they employed. The same happened in the United States and Canada, the latter finally forcing Britain to break off trade relations with Russia at the end of 1932. In France, agitation over Soviet dumping may have been exaggerated, given the overall pattern of French exports, but it took place in an atmosphere already poisoned by the ferment stirred up at the Comintern's support for the revolt in Indochina earlier in 1930. The result was the imposition of severe trade restrictions against the USSR, which lasted until French fears of a revanchist Germany led to a toning down of hitherto virulent anti-Sovietism.[7] Other countries had followed France's example – Belgium, Luxembourg, Yugoslavia and Romania – and the great danger for the Russians was that a global embargo on trade with the USSR might materialise, thereby wrecking any hope that the five-year plan could be completed within its allotted span. This left the country vulnerable for a much greater period than Stalin and his colleagues had bargained for.

The Soviets responded with a combination of firmness and diplomacy. Soon after the French imposed their trade restrictions, the Russians retaliated with an embargo of their own.[8] At the same time Litvinov unearthed the traditional offering of the non-aggression pact in novel form: economic non-aggression. This was then laid before the commission on European union at Geneva on the 18 May 1931. Litvinov argued that just as war was no way out of the world economic crisis, neither was "economic aggression". He called on states to join in a commitment not to adopt measures which would discriminate against the economy of any particular Power.[9] Unfortunately for the Russians, this delicate vine withered in the same frost which was slowly but surely killing proposals for disarmament (another recipient of Russian favours). But it did at least demonstrate to a Western public, fed on fearsome tales of how the Soviets were deliberately sabotaging economic recovery, that Moscow was not all evil.

The Russians were also counting on the fact that the negative impact of their exports would be more than offset by the positive effect of their imports from the West. At a time when domestic demand for their manufactures was rapidly falling, Western industrialists welcomed the Russians with their shopping lists – "it is a fact that we 'put water in their mill'", as Stalin remarked.[10] For countries such as Germany, suffering acute social and political turmoil as a result of the Depression, this was no small matter. The choice that confronted Berlin was either to trade with the Soviet Union or turn yet more workers onto the streets, where agitation for revolution was rife; and Moscow was not averse to reminding German capitalists of that fact.[11] Elsewhere in the West the situation may have been less desperate, but the growth of a pro-Soviet industrial lobby none the less proved significant in counteracting agitation for an embargo against Russian products.[12]

The other notable effect which the five-year plan had upon Moscow's foreign relations was to raise the regime's prestige in the eyes of friend and foe alike. These were the first signs of a process which saw its apogee in the widespread admiration of the USSR amongst large sections of the Western intelligentsia in the mid- to late-thirties. With the first plan only in its infancy, the process had just begun. Disbelief that an economy could be planned – and in Russia – was rapidly ebbing. Russian success in this field certainly won grudging respect, if nothing more, from those now only too conscious that their own social and economic order had come to grief with the Depression. The British ambassador to Moscow has provided us with his impressions, which illustrate this reaction. Referring to the changes in British public opinion that had occurred during the six months ending in July 1930, he reflected that "whatever the prejudice or the political anxiety that might arise from a dislike of Bolshevik methods, the experiment in itself is one of the most important and most far reaching that has ever been undertaken".[13]

Nor was it overlooked in Moscow that the USSR's prestige would also grow amongst the working classes of the West. Here was an important potential ally – in 1920 British dockers had refused to load arms for shipment to Poland which was then at war with the Russians. It was therefore not merely a matter of traditional internationalist sentiment when the Soviet Communist Party called for "the reinforcement of fraternal ties and solidarity of the workers and toiling masses of the USSR with the workers and toilers of capitalist countries and colonies".[14] The achievements of the five-year plan were extolled beyond belief in the pages of foreign Communist newspapers, like the *Daily Worker* in Britain. In a sense Communists abroad were using the Soviet Union as an advertisement for their own party. The Soviets were evidently content with this – flattering as it undoubtedly was – provided, in their turn, these Communists were also prepared to mobilise their followers to serve the Russian cause. The coincidence of the five-year plan with the onset of the Depression obviously helped the Soviet Union by enabling it to contrast its own full employment economy with the massive unemployment in the West. In other respects, however, the Depression proved to be of dubious benefit to the Soviet Union: it represented both new opportunities and new dangers.

At the sixth Comintern congress in 1928 there had been much loose talk about a new era of revolutions – an end to the stabilisation of capitalism that had characterised the 1920s– which was singularly inappropriate to the year in which it was proclaimed.[15] But with the Great Crash in 1929 it seemed to many that the capitalist world was, indeed, on the verge of collapse, and that the spectre of revolution would once again haunt Europe. However, in Moscow unbridled enthusiasm at the prospect of revolution was frequently counter-balanced by anxiety at the likely backlash this would engender in the West against the USSR. At crucial moments, ever doubtful about the ability of even the German Communist Party to succeed, the Soviet leadership reined the Comintern back from the edge of the precipice. When militants perceived the moment to be ripe, a fog of words suddenly enveloped the Comintern, as in the spring of 1930, with Germany in crisis:

The faster the crisis in capitalist stabilisation develops, the broader that the scope of development of the world labour movement becomes, the closer the perspective of proletarian revolution in a range of capitalist countries and of anti-imperialist bourgeois democratic revolution in the colonies and semi-colonies, the more complicated and onerous are the tasks of the international revolution's leaders – the Comintern and its individual sections.[16]

If Moscow had to restrain the Communists in Germany, elsewhere the problem was the reverse – most sections of the Comintern were losing support and falling into a dispirited apathy. This scarcely served Soviet interests either, and it is revealing that the French Communists were most severely rebuked for their inactivity on the anti-war front rather than for anything else; this was a time when the greatest danger to Soviet security came from France and its allies.[17]

To say that Communist Parties were, on the whole, signally failing to become significant forces within their societies does not, however, mean that the Depression left the West as stable as it had been before. On the contrary, unrest was rife. But mass unemployment spawned Fascism rather than Communism. Instead of becoming an era of revolutions, it fast became an era of counter-revolutions, and although the Soviet leadership thought that it could harness these forces to its own advantage, it underestimated both their strength and their commitment to old-fashioned anti-Sovietism.

The Soviet leadership's attitude towards Fascism was dictated by overriding fears that Europe would be stabilised under French hegemony. It had been a vital element in Soviet foreign policy since its earliest days under Lenin, to exploit the tensions and antagonisms which beset relations amongst the capitalist Powers. As hostility towards the USSR was taken as given, any unification of the Western Powers represented a menace to Soviet security, even if the states concerned were as insignificant as the little kingdoms in the Balkans.[18] Moscow felt very strongly that only with the Western Powers at one another's throats – though not at war – would the USSR be secure.

Germany's integration into the Western camp was in danger of leaving the USSR isolated from Europe. The process of whittling away the significance of the Rapallo relationship between Berlin and Moscow, which began with the Locarno Pact in 1925, looked like reaching its culmination with Germany's acceptance of the Young plan for reparations payments in 1929. Moscow saw it as vital to maintain the divide between Germany and the Western

Powers. The German Communists attacked the plan, as did the Fascists. Only the Social Democrats and the Centre Party accepted its conditions. Obsessed with Germany's drift westwards the Soviet leadership was blind to the menace the Fascists represented and, despite warnings from senior Soviet diplomats, Stalin and the Politburo pursued a course which ultimately contributed to a situation in which Hitler's accession to power became a reality.[19]

In the East the Depression precipitated Japanese aggression against China in September 1931, which came to represent the most immediate threat to Soviet security that Moscow had experienced for many years. The simultaneous disruption of both industry and defence caused by excessive rates of growth and agricultural collectivisation left the Russians with no real protection against attack from Japan. The fear that Tokyo might ally with the USSR's adversaries in the West also haunted Soviet thinking throughout these troubled years. The Americans, upon whom the Russians initially placed such great hopes as a buttress against Japanese expansionism, proved a disappointment; and even US diplomatic recognition proved unattainable until December 1933. The Russians were on their own.

2 The Conduct of Soviet Diplomacy

Despite the turbulence of these years in the Soviet Union, power remained essentially in the hands of Stalin, provided he continued to maintain a minimal consensus amongst his immediate entourage in the leadership. His main preoccupation, however, was not with foreign affairs – until their intrusion could no longer be ignored – but with the awesome task of recasting Russia as a modern, industrialised Power. Thus whereas Stalin and his cohorts in the Politburo reserved for themselves alone the highest decisions of state, in foreign policy, at least, a large share of the responsibility was delegated to the specialists and, in the case of diplomacy, to the officials at the Commissariat for Foreign Affairs – the Narkomindeltsy.

At the pinnacle of this pyramid sat the Commissar who, according to the constitution, acted as chairman of and spokesman for the Narkomindel collegium – a collective body composed exclusively of the institution's most senior figures. These included the two Deputy Commissars: one for the Western world, the other overseeing the East. The Deputy Commissar for the West was the more senior of the two and substituted for the Commissar in his absence – holidays were staggered for this purpose. It was in this manner that Maxim Litvinov came to displace Georgii Chicherin as Commissar in the late 1920s. For the chronic deterioration in his health meant that Chicherin came to spend increasingly extended periods abroad recuperating in the spas of Central Europe, thus causing him to lose his grip on the workings of the Commissariat.[1] Thus, as *Izvestiya* noted on the 17 July 1936, Litvinov became "the de facto head of our foreign policy from 1928",[2] despite Chicherin's formal retention of the post until the summer of 1930. This transition also coincided with Stalin's accession to supreme power and the two processes were not unconnected, as *Pravda* explained some thirty years later:

10

G.V.Chicherin boldly spoke out against the mistaken views of Stalin, Rykov and Bukharin on an array of international political questions, including the issue of aid to the countries of the East.

In 1930 Chicherin was removed from the post of People's Commissar for Foreign Affairs. The reason for his dismissal was not merely illness, but also Stalin's resentment at Chicherin's critical remarks.[3]

His successor Litvinov (né Moishe Wallach) was born on the 17 July (new style) 1876 in Byalistok, the son of a Jewish bank clerk. Like others of his generation in the Russian empire, he was swept up by the wave of unrest in the 1890s, and before the decade was out he had begun his career as "a professional revolutionary". He joined the Russian Social Democratic Labour Party (RSDLP) in 1898 and his activities within it soon led to imprisonment and finally exile. Unlike Chicherin, he sided with the Bolsheviks after the RSDLP split in 1903. Arrested on a mission in France five years later, he was deported to Britain, where he stayed for the next decade, for the greater part of which he headed the emigré Bolshevik group and represented his party at the bureau of the Socialist International.[4] It was during this period that he met and later (1917) married Ivy Low, the daughter of a Jewish university professor.[5] On the day after the Bolsheviks seized power in Russia the Sovnarkom (Council of People's Commissars) appointed him its plenipotentiary (polpred) in Britain. He was subsequently arrested, ostensibly for addressing public meetings to oppose the allied war of intervention, and his release was obtained only when the Russians seized Bruce-Lockhart, Britain's unofficial emissary to Moscow, and offered an exchange.[6] Arriving in the new Soviet capital at the end of 1918, he was appointed to the Narkomindel collegium and was immediately despatched to Stockholm, where he issued an unsuccessful appeal for peace. Deported from Sweden, he reappeared abroad in 1919 when he brought off his first diplomatic coup, by concluding an agreement with a number of countries (including Britain and France) on the exchange of prisoners of war. At a crucial moment the Bolsheviks had secured the opening of de facto diplomatic relations with the Allies. From then on Litvinov's rise was certain. In 1921, with the expansion of the Narkomindel following the spread of international recognition, he was appointed first Deputy Commissar.

As a diplomat Litvinov had none of Chicherin's charm and sophistication, though he had other qualities to recommend him, as Count Grandi, the Italian Foreign Minister, noted after their first encounter in late November 1930:

> He gives the impression of being a cultivated man, quick and nimble-witted. He displays remarkable knowledge of and feel for international problems not limited to that which directly interests his country. He appears to be well-informed. His logic is simplistic, crude and lacks finesse.[7] He gives the impression of being a politician of a certain stature, endowed with shrewdness, who nevertheless lacks the resources for the art of diplomacy.[8]

In fact Litvinov proved a more successful diplomat than Grandi, and those aspects of Litvinov's manner which rubbed so uneasily with an aristocratic Italian sensibility mattered little in the rough milieu of Stalin's Moscow; if anything they were an asset. And although British diplomats, too, found him coarse and sarcastic, they also appreciated his frankness and general comprehension of the West.[9] For whilst Chicherin was cosmopolitan in manner, he was strongly anti-Western in outlook, whereas Litvinov was precisely the reverse. There were other important differences, too. Although Litvinov was the old Bolshevik and his predecessor the ex-Menshevik, Chicherin was the one more given to standing by his revolutionary principles, in contrast to Litvinov's *"great sense of realism"*.[10] Their respective attitudes towards disarmament illustrate this fundamental difference in outlook.

In 1922, with preparations for the Genoa conference under way, Lenin wanted the Soviet delegation to advocate disarmament in order to win over bourgeois pacifist sentiment in the West, even at the expense of misleading the workers. Chicherin was shocked at this and only yielded to Lenin's instructions with the greatest distaste.[11] Litvinov, on the other hand, found nothing wrong with the idea. On the contrary, he was ready to try anything, as Louis Fischer has pointed out:

> Litvinov's foreign policy was to avoid trouble. Truest revolutionary, he wished to keep Russia at peace so it could develop internally. He did not want to spend money on a Red

fleet, he told me. He sought to develop Soviet foreign trade. He endeavoured to enhance Moscow's prestige by Soviet participation in conferences, pacts and agreements. Disarmament at Geneva was his "baby". Chicherin never liked it. Assistant Commissar Litvinov fought for Soviet adherence to the Kellogg pact. Chicherin, the Commissar, fought against this. The Soviets adhered. It did no good, and Litvinov did not expect war to be outlawed. But he wanted Moscow to appear on the world stage.[12]

These differences in outlook and temperament were also reflected in their administration of the Narkomindel, as Maisky, one-time polpred in London, describes. It did not merely mean an end to the notorious habit Chicherin engendered of working at night, when Litvinov took over:

Georgii Vasil'evich [Chicherin] one way or another spontaneously tried to concentrate all the work, even down to trifles, in his own hands. As a result, he frequently had clashes and conflicts with colleagues, even the most powerful. As a result, relations between Chicherin and Litvinov, in particular, were never smooth. They respected one another, they understood that their working together was necessary in the interests of the party and state, but it was not easy.

The methods of running the Commissariat under Maxim Maximovich [Litvinov] were different. To be sure, he wished to be and in fact was the real head of his department; however, Litvinov knew how to farm out work amongst his colleagues in the proper manner and encouraged initiative and independence, leaving for himself merely any checking and correction that proved necessary. This was especially evident in relations between the Commissar and polpreds. He frequently told them: the Commissariat gives you general directives on serious questions, your job is to know how to translate these directives into practice – that's why you have a brain in your head; don't burden the Commissariat with trifles, it needs the time for more important matters.[13]

Though these "efficient management methods" were undoubtedly much appreciated by his subordinates,[14] the other side to the picture was that, in contrast to Chicherin's regime, relations between the Commissar and polpreds tended to be "strictly business-like".[15] There was evidently none of the personal interest which Chicherin displayed towards some of his subordinates in his final years.[16]

So much for Litvinov's leadership of the Narkomindel; but what of his relations with Stalin and the Politburo? By the beginning of 1930 it was already apparent that Chicherin would have to go, and not merely because of Stalin's dislike for him. His health had broken down completely. In the grip of a severe form of polyneuritis, he was unable to rest without recourse to morphine and other narcotics. As a result, and after consultations with the Kremlin's doctors, the party leadership apparently met on the 16 January to consider a suitable replacement. Word had it that Litvinov threatened to resign from the Narkomindel should its leadership pass into anyone else's hands.[17] It is said that he was "driven by a wily and at times brutal kind of ambition",[18] and was, as Krestinsky noted, "an emotional man",[19] so such rumours are not implausible. Indeed, Krestinsky, then polpred in Berlin, was rumoured to be the most likely alternative candidate to Litvinov and, according to Italian diplomatic sources (particularly close to the Narkomindel at this time), the Politburo, reluctant to precipitate anything which might cast a shadow over the prestige of the USSR abroad, decided to shelve the matter for the time being.[20] Henceforth a spate of rumours began to circulate as to Chicherin's likely successor. Kirov, Rykov, Andreev and Mikoyan were all named as possible contenders. All they had in common was their ignorance of foreign lands and foreign languages. Evidently at least a part of the resistance to Litvinov's appointment can be explained by the deep mistrust of the Narkomindel within the party, for not only was it liberally staffed with Jews, it was also almost exclusively made up of those who had been emigrés under Tsarist rule, unlike the current generation of party leaders and their cadres.[21] The Workers' and Peasants' Inspectorate (Rabkrin), the government's new broom, had already swept its way through other departments of state, purging them of unreliable and independent-minded elements.[22] Although the Narkomindel had been praised by Lenin in the early days as the best of all Commissariats,[23] it had since greatly expanded, and such a compliment meant little now in these changed times. The dismissal of Fyodor Rotshtein from his position at the head of the Narkomindel press department early in 1930, apparently for excessive liberalism, was a straw in the wind.[24] There were two other likely reasons for opposition to Litvinov's appointment, both of which were to dog his progress as Commissar throughout the thirties. Firstly, his "strength of character"[25] – as Krestinsky noted, and clearly not merely with reference to his country's adversaries: "In a fight, comrade Litvinov gives no quarter to the enemy";[26] others were also struck by his "inflexible will"[27] and his "firmness and implacability in pursuit of his aims".[28] He was, as Krestinsky wrote, "a born fighter".[29] Secondly he was a known Anglophile, and this ran counter to the pro-German profile of Soviet foreign policy since Rapallo (1922). The choice between Litvinov and Krestinsky, even given the Politburo's ultimate control over the direction of diplomacy, undoubtedly had some significance for the orientation of Moscow's foreign policy – as events were later to demonstrate.

The notion of a last-minute decision with respect to Litvinov's appointment[30] is given added weight by the fact that at least since 1925 this post was buttressed by simultaneous membership of the party central committee. Yet the XVI party congress met in June 1930 leaving Litvinov without this necessary adjunct to his political stature. Thus his appointment as Commissar, announced on the 22 July, left him without any formal place in the party hierarchy, until the XVII congress rectified the anomaly in January 1934. One suspects that Stalin's motive for leaving the Commissariat in Litvinov's hands probably stemmed from the wish to avoid giving a crucial post to anyone who might become a serious political rival (this is evident until 1953). Litvinov was suitable not merely for his experience, his undoubted talents and Stalin's ability to get along with him, but also due to his total political impotence within the party.

Below Litvinov was the collegium. In July 1930 it now included Litvinov's two rivals, Nikolai Krestinsky and Lev Karakhan. A further addition was the more junior Boris Stomonyakov, known to be one of the Commissar's protegés. Let us turn to Krestinsky first: born on the 25 October 1883 into the family of a secondary-school teacher in Byelorussia, he had joined the RSDLP in 1903, participated in the 1905 revolution and worked as a lawyer for the Bolsheviks who sat in the Duma, thus precipitating his sure persecution by the authorities. In 1917, after the fall of the Tsar, he headed the Bolshevik party organisation in the Urals, his place of exile, and with the success of the October revolution he became Commissar of Justice for the Northern Commune area and subsequently Commissar of Finance for the RSFSR. From the end of 1919 until March 1921, he then acted as a secretary to the party central committee. But he was no conformist – opposing the signature of the Brest-Litovsk treaty and siding with the joint Trotsky-Bukharin opposition on trade union issues in 1921 until, probably as a result, he was sent as polpred to Berlin that same year. This preventive measure, if indeed this is what it was, did not prove a total success, however. For he then joined the united opposition platform (against Stalin and Bukharin) in 1927 and not until well after its defeat did he return to the fold. That this degree of recalcitrance brought him no immediate retribution was undoubtedly due to the fact that these very energies which made him so troublesome to the dominant faction in the Kremlin were also successfully channelled into serving existing Soviet state interests in Berlin, the most crucial diplomatic posting of them all, where he served as the lynchpin of the Rapallo relationship between Weimar Germany and Soviet Russia.[31]

His colleague Lev Karakhan (né Karakhanyan) was born in Tbilisi on the 1 or 2 February 1889,[32] into the family of a lawyer, then of some renown in the Caucasus. His career as a revolutionary dates from 1904 when he joined the RSDLP, moving to Harbin (1905) and then on to Vladivostok along with his father, who had been obliged to leave Georgia as a result of his liberal views. In 1910 Karakhan went to Petrograd, hoping to enrol in the university's low faculty. But failing the entrance examinations, he found work as a correspondent for city newspapers, the legal counterpart to his underground work which in 1915 caused his arrest and deportation to Siberia. After the February revolution he returned to the capital and by October 1917 was a member of the presidium and secretary of the Petrograd soviet. He, along with others from his group – the Mezhraiontsy – joined the Bolsheviks en masse just prior to the October rising. As a member of the military-revolutionary committee he helped organise the coup which brought the Bolsheviks to power, and was then sent as a representative of the committee to negotiate peace with the Germans.

This marks the beginning of his life as a diplomat. In March 1918, as a reward for his efforts, he became Deputy Commissar for Foreign Affairs and in April the following year formally took charge of Eastern policy. In 1923 to 1924 it was Karakhan who conducted the delicate negotiations establishing diplomatic relations with China, where he remained as head of the Soviet mission. Here he fell victim to Litvinov's longstanding dispute with Chicherin. The latter was taking a cure abroad and, on learning of Karakhan's arrival in Moscow, wrote urging him to resume control over oriental affairs. Chicherin also asked the Narkomindel collegium to accept Karakhan as his substitute for the time being. This rather crude attempt to prevent Litvinov from assuming control over the Commissariat backfired when Litvinov succeeded in obtaining Karakhan's recall to Peking when the revolution in China suddenly cascaded "like snow"[33] onto their heads. Nonetheless even as polpred in Peking Karakhan retained his title as Deputy Commissar, and after his return in August 1926 played an active part in the development of Soviet policy in the East, before Litvinov finally succeeded in having him removed from the levers of power.

Differences between the two were only accentuated by the Japanese assault on Manchuria in the autumn of 1931. Towards the end of 1932 Litvinov suggested that Karakhan return to China as polpred, now that diplomatic relations had been re-established (after the breach in 1929), but this met with a refusal.[34] A turning point came in the spring of 1933 when the issue arose of selling the Chinese Eastern Railway to the Japanese. It is significant that the decision to sell was announced to the press (in rather defensive language) by Litvinov, rather than Karakhan,[35] and just over a fortnight later (evidently to dissociate the two events in the public mind) on the 25 May Sokol'nikov was appointed Deputy Commissar, and it soon emerged that he was taking over Karakhan's responsibilities for the Far East.[36] Then a year later, when the collegiate system was abolished in all Commissariats, Karakhan lost his post as Deputy Commissar altogether and was banished to the embassy in Ankara.[37]

Litvinov's hostility, evidently a combination of the personal and the political, stood in stark contrast to the views of others. The British ambassador, for one, found him "extremely affable" and "more at ease and more a man of the world than either Litvinov or Stomonyakov".[38] Chicherin admired him for his quick mind, his good judgement and outstanding flair for politics.[39] And the former diplomat Barmine remembered him with some affection and not merely for his stunningly good looks, but also as a "born optimist, a conscientious worker, simple in his dealings with others, and always ready to give a helping hand to his younger colleagues".[40]

The fourth member of the team, Boris Stomonyakov, is something of an enigma. A Jew like Litvinov, he was born in 1882, the son of a Russian nobleman employed as an officer in the Bulgarian army. It would appear that he was raised in Russia, for after joining the RSDLP in 1902, he was deported from the country two years later. From then on his revolutionary activities continued in exile until, for some unknown reason, he abandoned them completely in Berlin (1910). World War I saw him serving in the Bulgarian army (against the Russians) until in 1917 he was transferred to work at the Bulgarian embassy in the Netherlands. He then resigned at the end of the war and moved to Germany where he began to work for the Bolsheviks, becoming their trade representative in Berlin from 1921 to 1924. On moving to the Soviet Union he worked in the Narkomindel's legal department until, with Litvinov's backing, he took charge of relations with Poland and the Baltic states, joining the collegium in 1926.[41] Soviet sources tell us nothing of his character, but the British found him "affable, intelligent, talkative",[42] whilst the Italians considered him "cold, hard and reserved";[43] however this may tell us more about the British or the Italians, or alternatively whom Stomonyakov preferred as company.

The question that now arises is the extent of their influence over foreign policy. Formally the Soviet Government as such was distinct from the Communist Party proper and its leaders in the Politburo. In practice, however, all major policy decisions were settled within the Politburo and this applied to foreign relations as much as anything else. The chairman of the Council of People's Commissars (Sovnarkom) was, from the end of 1930, Molotov, a member of the Politburo and a close associate of Stalin; so there was considerable overlap between the state and party structures at the top. But Stalin himself appears, at least from the documents now available, to have only rarely taken a direct hand in the day-to-day running of diplomacy; it was simply not his forte, and his own personal secretariat which grew up at this time does not, in foreign affairs at least,[44] appear to have exerted any great influence over policy. In general Soviet missions abroad communicated directly with the Narkomindel; the collegium handled the more important material and the Commissar was in overall control. Stalin rarely conducted his own correspondence with Soviet diplomats abroad and did so only when he thought matters were of supreme importance.[45] Even when the Commissar was on business elsewhere – and Litvinov was jokingly referred to as "a citizen of Geneva" – he would normally write to his Deputy, usually Krestinsky, who would then inform the Politburo, and vice versa.[46]

The Narkomindel's influence over the leadership's policy decisions came from informed recommendation rather than political muscle, a practice little different from the diplomatic service in any Western capital. The fact that diplomatic tactics, as opposed to grand strategy, were generally left to the discretion of the specialist undoubtedly gave the latter the opportunity to create faits accomplis which the leadership could reverse only with difficulty without damaging the country's prestige; and Stalin usually knew when to leave well enough alone.[47] Indeed, although Litvinov never entirely had his own way – particularly over Germany, both in the period currently under discussion, with respect to the dangers Fascism portended for Russia, and in the future with Fascism in power[48] – it was nevertheless also true that Soviet diplomacy bore his unmistakable imprint.

In enumerating the policies pursued abroad by the Soviet Union from 1928 till 1936 (the time of his writing), Krestinsky wrote:

> As our economic and military power grew, comrade Litvinov, in complete accordance with the directives of the CC of our party and the direct instructions of our leader comrade Stalin, went on to the diplomatic offensive and added a succession of new pages to the history of international relations linked to the name of the Soviet Union and its unchanging representative in the international arena, comrade Litvinov.[49]

It is seemingly a paradox that whereas Stalin was temperamentally an isolationist in foreign policy, his Commissar for Foreign Affairs was unmistakably an internationalist. Yet Stalin's extreme suspiciousness and defensiveness towards the outside world was more than counterbalanced by two further qualities, which led him to abstain from constant and direct involvement in the conduct of foreign relations. Firstly he was above all a realist – a feature he shared with Litvinov – and this realism extended to

Stalin's assessment of his own capabilities; ignorant of foreign affairs, he generally left such issues to competent subordinates. Secondly, Stalin was always prone to let matters drift, preferring to delay decision whilst events took their course and until the situation had clarified sufficiently to allow for a definitive judgement. This frequently left a vacuum which others could fill. It sometimes meant that standing debates were left unresolved, that contradictory policies could be pursued simultaneously and that decisions taken below could suddenly be reversed by unexpected intervention from above. This ensured that Soviet foreign policy was anything but monolithic.

3 1930: Crises at Home and Abroad

The year 1930 proved a period of trials in both Soviet domestic and foreign policies. The crisis in agricultural collectivisation unfortunately coincided with a series of crises in the USSR's foreign relations, leaving the country not only weaker than before, but also dangerously isolated, and exposed to pressures from abroad. For, whilst exciting exaggerated fears of Russia's growing power in neighbouring states, Stalin's "revolution from above" simultaneously failed to meet its own objectives at home: a near fatal combination for any regime. Yet none of this was apparent at the outset.

There were a number of reasons for this, both domestic and foreign. Firstly, the Bolsheviks were liquidating capitalist agriculture, and with it the forces most opposed to socialism in Russia and "the last base" of foreign intervention.[1] Secondly, the implementation of the five-year plan heralded a strong industrial infrastructure for Russia, promising not only greater economic self-sufficiency but also military power to match that of potential adversaries. Industry was booming, as vast and hitherto un-employed resources were sucked into the giant machinery of construction.[2] On the international front, the omens were equally good. The Depression appeared to signal disaster for the fabric of capitalist society. The growth of working-class unrest was already apparent. "World imperialism is beginning to worry seriously about its rear", *Pravda* claimed,[3] and this applied to the colonies as much as the metropolis; for in the dependent territories lay the "multi-million reserves of the proletarian revolution", so Moscow believed.[4] Apparently no one had given much thought to the likely backlash this would cause, threatening the stability of the USSR's hard-won co-existence with the West.

In terms of concrete achievements, the Soviets could cite the renewal of diplomatic relations with Britain on the 30 October

21

1929.[5] The diplomatic set-back caused by Britain's breach of relations in 1927 was now reversed, and this was a highly valued prize, for Britain was still considered the leading Power in Europe. It also appeared to be the first solid sign that the capitalist world was taking the five-year plan seriously. For although the resumption of relations was initiated by a Labour Government, it had the backing of not only the Liberal Party, but also important manufacturing interests. A British industrial mission visited the USSR in late March 1929; they were not only much impressed by what they saw, but also by the blunt language which greeted them. *"In the event of our relations with England remaining unregulated, the USSR's imports from England will be limited only to the most negligible and absolutely necessary quantities, which are impossible to calculate in advance"*, warned Pyatakov, chairman of the Soviet State Bank and head of the Soviet delegation.[6] The industrial mission returned to Britain "satisfied that there is a great volume of business available for Great Britain, subject to diplomatic recognition being afforded, and if arrangements be made for the financing of the business on long term credit or otherwise".[7]

A further filip to Moscow's spirits resulted from swift and successful action against Chiang Kai-shek's troops in November 1929, for the repossession of the Chinese Eastern Railway; a strategic route which provided the Russians with direct access to the interior of Manchuria.[8] However, the ramifications of this action were shortly to be felt in Europe, where the Soviet victory alarmed not only the Poles, but also their French allies, and the resultant state of agitation added unnecessarily to the burdens faced by the Soviet leadership in the spring of 1930. In the longer term it also contributed to the causes of Japanese expansion into Manchuria from the autumn of 1931, by further unsettling the Kwantung Army Command, already nervous about the future security of Japanese interests in the area. But at the beginning of 1930 all this was impossible to foresee. Soviet leaders had no reason then to doubt that Russia's star was in the ascendant.

The tenor of Soviet press comment on the international situation reflected this feeling of ebullient self-confidence. The capitalist Powers were in disarray. Speculating on the outcome of the London Naval Conference, due to convene on the 23 January, *Izvestiya* forecast failure. Referring to the positions of the various Powers concerned – Britain, France, Italy, Japan and the United

States – it argued that "the conflicting proposals ... have very little chance of being translated into reality".[9] Similarly, in assessing the achievements of the second Hague conference, which opened on the 3 January to solve outstanding questions on German reparations, the newspaper insisted that "all the old disagreements were exacerbated and to those new ones were added".[10] The counterpart to crowing over the disorder in the capitalist camp was the belligerent attitude adopted towards any who threatened Soviet interests. The Mexican Government's breach of diplomatic relations with the Soviet Union, announced tactlessly and prematurely to the press on the 24 January, before Moscow had officially been informed, merely aroused *Izvestiya*'s contempt.[11] Mexico was a lightweight on the international scales; however, the Soviet attitude towards France was no less self-assured when a crisis suddenly broke out that same month.

On the 26 January OGPU agents had spirited away General Kutepov, leader of the Russian counter-revolutionaries centred in Paris.[12] As far as the rest of the world was aware (including the French police), he had simply disappeared.[13] But the emigré Russian community was certain that he had been abducted by the Soviets, and before long enlisted the services of the French press to make the case a cause célèbre.[14] Holidaying in the south of France with his wife when the crisis broke, Deputy Commissar Krestinsky found the climate changing suddenly from the mild to the malevolent.[15] Meanwhile in Paris his compatriots at the embassy, largely ignorant of OGPU planning, were left to face the unpleasant consequences.[16] "The situation may become serious", polpred Dovgalevsky informed Moscow. "Tardieu is in London, Briand has returned for only a few days. The Government in fact has no head. It is possible that anti-Soviet forces will attempt to use this anarchy to create an atmosphere conducive to a breach of relations".[17] With threatening letters arriving in the post, the Soviet mission went into a state of siege. Dovgalevsky set about organising the defence of the building against "surprise attack" by vengeful emigrés. Yet in Moscow the reaction was one of indignation rather than fright. An editorial appeared in *Izvestiya* aggressively entitled "Where is M. Tardieu's Government?", and put the following ultimatum to the Tardieu-Briand Cabinet: "does the French Government prefer the maintenance of diplomatic relations with the government of the Soviet Union to co-operation with white guard emigrés?", adding ominously that "normal diplomatic relations are incompatible with that sort of thing".[18]

Throughout the 1920s Moscow had panicked at the thought that any Great Power might contemplate a breach of relations, yet now the Russians felt sufficiently confident to threaten others. In relation to Germany they showed a similar defiance. A trial held in Berlin from the 6 January to the 8 February ended in acquittal or amnesty for all those involved in forging Soviet currency. The Soviet press here too demanded answers. Did the German Government expect that such a decision could "leave the USSR's political and economic relations with Germany unaffected?", *Izvestiya* warned; "actions" were needed and "not just words".[19]

These seemingly sturdy pillars of self-confidence began to crumble early in February with the sudden realisation that the USSR's rivals were by no means as divided as the Russians had supposed. This discovery coincided with a crisis in the collectivisation of agriculture, which threatened to bring the USSR to the verge of civil war. Foreign diplomats in Moscow soon sensed the sudden growth of apprehension amongst Soviet officials. The British ambassador first became aware of this early in February, but was initially inclined to dismiss it as mere "fireworks" rather than a real fire.[20] However, by the end of March he was convinced that these fears were genuine even if, as he strongly and correctly believed, they were fundamentally unjustified.[21] The Italian ambassador, too, was surprised by the "high level of anxiety on the part of the Commissariat for Foreign Affairs about the 'grave' international situation facing the USSR". An official with whom he had been in contact over several days insisted that "once again there was an attempt to build a united anti-Soviet front with the aim of attacking the Moscow Government militarily and of smashing Communism".[22]

This new sense of alarm also found its way into the press. On the 10 February an article appeared in the Comintern journal *Kommunisticheskii Internatsional*. Entitled "Internecine Strife Among the Imperialists and the Preparation of War Against the USSR", it reassessed the results of the London Naval Conference in the light of the growing anti-Soviet campaign in Europe:

. . . there is a real possibility of a softening, if only temporarily, of all the sharpening contradictions among the imperialist

Powers. This will naturally hasten the attempt of these Powers to come to terms on the one question on which they can establish a united front – the question of the USSR. For the implacable hatred of the only proletarian state in the world itself acts as cement. Only with the help of this can the imperialists hope to fill in the cracks which threaten new internecine imperialist conflicts in the immediate future.

Ironically the very factors which previously had inspired so much confidence were now mobilised to explain what lay behind the new danger of war:

> the five-year plan, the collective farm movement, the processes of industrialisation and collectivisation of agriculture developing at an unprecedented pace mean that in the course of the next few years the economy of the Soviet Union will finally and irrevocably liquidate the capitalist elements. These processes will put an end to all capitalist hopes for the 'regeneration' of the Bolsheviks and the restoration of capitalism on Soviet soil. Imperialism, dreaming about the destruction of the Soviet system or of forcing it to capitulate, evidently considers that it is in danger of being too late. Hence the tendency to put the question: now or never. This way of expressing it is also facilitated by those temporary and specific conditions which have arisen by the very fact of rapid socialist reconstruction and which favour plans for intervention. In particular, the imperialists are undoubtedly counting on the presence of about a million kulak households in the process of liquidation in the Soviet Union.[23]

Behind these fears lay a genuine and growing concern at the impact of collectivisation on the country's soldiery. As early as the 4 February *Krasnaya Zvezda*, the armed forces newspaper, emphasised that "the political organs of the army must show maximum initiative, flexibility and ability to resist the influence of the kulak, which will continue to infiltrate the barracks". This is surely what War Commissar Voroshilov had in mind when he stated that "the past year was a year of great trials and testing not only for the military training of the Red Army, but also for its *moral-political* stability".[24] The military leadership were worried at the army's participation in what was fast appearing a disastrous enterprise, drawing its attention from its primary role at a time when international tension had risen to unexpected heights.[25] It was at this point – in late February – that the military press became more explicit about the crisis within the armed forces. With unusual candour, the Red Army journal *Voennyi Vestnik* referred to "some comrades" who failed to understand why the kulak had to be liquidated, and these included members of "party organisations". "Opportunists" within the army were going so far as to defend the kulaks. One party member insisted that "the kulak was a revolutionary force" and another asked "why liquidate the kulak when he's of use to us" – "as though the proletarian state is not an organ for the liberation of the toiling masses from the yoke of capitalism, but a department of social insurance for capitalists", the journal commented sarcastically.[26]

Further complications now arose. A war scare began to envelop neighbouring Romania with the claim (which the Soviets knew to be fraudulent) that Russian forces were mobilising along the Romanian frontier. The precise origins of this canard are difficult to trace. It would appear to have arisen in response to speculation from the French embassy in Moscow, further elaborated in Paris and Warsaw. The French, the Poles and the Romanians were linked in an alliance system, one vital aim of which was to prevent the expansion of Soviet power westwards. There were no diplomatic relations between Romania and the USSR because of Romania's annexation of Bessarabia and Russian unwillingness to accept its loss. In Moscow both the Polish and French embassies had been alarmed by the Red Army's successful strike into Manchuria in November 1929 and Herbette, the French ambassador, a rather impulsive spirit little suited to diplomacy, readily convinced himself that the Russians would attack Eastern Europe. He therefore twisted all incoming information to reinforce this assumption. For instance, the Soviets had announced that two of their warships which left Naples in mid-January were not returning to the Baltic – where they belonged – but to Odessa, supposedly for repairs. Herbette firmly believed that this must be a ploy. The Turks should have shown some concern at the arrival of warships in the Black Sea and, seeing that they were indifferent, Herbette jumped to the conclusion that there was a Russo-Turkish entente. Logic then led him relentlessly on:

If one adds to these considerations other details (such as the numerous landing exercises carried out by the Soviet fleet in the Black Sea during the past year) one can not escape from the thought that the USSR's intentions towards Rumania appear to be less and less reassuring. Master of the Black Sea, secure on its Central Asian frontiers, and confident in the Power that borders the straits (through which military supplies arrive from Italy and through which the vessels of states friendly to Rumania must also pass), the government of the USSR would have no problem in dealing a blow at Bessarabia and Bukovina.

The present condition of the Red Army would prove no obstacle . . .

Obviously without allowing one to state that a conflict is either imminent or inevitable, this information suffices to show that the danger might materialise any day.[27]

The French and the Poles thus alerted the Romanians to the threat apparently emerging from Moscow. The Polish military attaché in Bucharest was instructed by his government "to use every means to induce the ROUMANIAN military authorities to strengthen their military defensive organisation in BESSARABIA". To this end he encouraged the opposition press to spread tales of an imminent Soviet attack.[28]

To the Russians the war scare could only be part of a plot to cover Romania's aggressive intentions. Litvinov wrote to Arosev, polpred in Prague, on the 28 February, suggesting that:

The hubbub has evidently been stirred up with the aim of strengthening the general anti-Soviet campaign and also, no doubt, to justify possible military preparations on the part of Romania.[29]

Such fears received plausible confirmation by reports early in March that the Romanians were holding "important manoeuvres" in a province bordering the Dnestr.[30] When combined with pressures from the Red Army high command, these anxieties undoubtedly played some part in Stalin's decision to retreat from the forced collectivisation of agriculture, thus reluctantly granting a further span of life to the "last base" for foreign intervention in the USSR.[31]

While all was proceeding well at home, foreign complications tended to diminish in significance. But now that their rear had become alarmingly insecure, the optimism of the Soviet leadership gave way to its opposite. The international situation looked increasingly menacing. At a time when it appeared that a collision with the Versailles Powers was in prospect, the Russians naturally turned to Germany as a counterbalance. But here too they began to feel dangerously isolated.

Since 1922 the USSR's security had been founded upon a bedrock of common interest shared with Germany, and the focal point of this relationship was hostility towards Poland. Thus the signature of a commercial agreement between Poland and Germany on the 17 March 1930, ending the tariff war waged since the late 1920s, came as an unpleasant reminder to the Russians of the precariousness of their international position. They interpreted this move as the product of Germany's drive for a lasting accommodation with the Allies – Britain, France and the USA – and not as in any sense related to the growing sense of frustration welling up in Berlin at Soviet involvement in Germany's internal affairs. The Russians were basically correct, but were at the same time wrong to underestimate the extent to which growing Communist agitation in Germany tended to reinforce Berlin's identification with the West rather than the East. Ever since the German Government had accepted the Young plan for reparations payments in return for Allied evacuation of the Rhineland, an agreement unhesitatingly condemned in Moscow,[32] the Russians increasingly drew hope from Germany's impending economic disintegration and social collapse. Reichswehr Minister Gröner had himself argued that Germany stood on the verge of "state bankruptcy" and predicted "disorder" in the event of Young plan payments being met by squeezing the economy still further.[33] The likely source of unrest was the German Communist Party (KPD), and its supporters did take to the streets. There were battles across the barricades in various cities. But the party had a membership less than half the size of 1923, the year of the last abortive revolution.[34] The Russians were only too aware that this was an inadequate army with which to stage a revolution; they therefore pulled on the reins when there was any likelihood of serious action.[35] At the same time, the

German security forces expressed confidence in their ability to contain whatever the Communists were able to threaten.[36] None the less the existing disruption was sufficient to aggravate relations with Russia. The German embassy in Moscow began "showering" the Narkomindel with protests, both verbal and written.[37] Within the Cabinet the Russian question was hotly debated and resolved in Moscow's favour only when Reichswehr Minister Gröner reproved those who suggested breaking with Moscow: "only relations with Russia give the army the opportunity to familiarise itself with the most modern weapons and to keep itself abreast of manufacturing processes", he argued successfully.[38] Here was Moscow's greatest ally, though for the moment the Russians were uncertain whether they might not soon be deserted. Relations between Berlin and Moscow were at their nadir. An article in the Narkomindel journal *Mezhdunarodnaya Zhizn'* caught this sense of bewildering uncertainty. In concluding a discussion of the German–Polish treaty "Germanikus" wrote that:

> The immediate future will reveal the direction in which German–Polish relations will develop and what distorting effects it will have on (*kak oni budut prelomlyat'sya na*) German foreign policy as a whole, and on German-Soviet relations in particular. The same future will reveal how well German foreign policy has followed the course given at the Versailles school.[39]

What made the Polish–German rapprochement even more disturbing was the loose talk in Warsaw of a preventive war against the USSR. The Polish Government was in fact innocent of such intentions, but it was also alarmed at the Red Army's victory in Manchuria and had convinced itself that domestic difficulties would before long catapult the Russians into a war of aggression in Eastern Europe. As a result the Polish general staff was instructed to base its planning on a new assumption: that the Soviet Union was a more immediate threat to their security than Germany.[40] Typically, the Russians had the same view of the Poles. An editorial in *Izvestiya* entitled "Poland and the USSR", which appeared on the 18 March, contained the following passages:

> A semi-official organ, the *Gazeta Polska*, has been devoting a

series of articles to our five-year plan, expressing the idea that if the USSR succeeds in carrying out its programme of construction unhindered, its power will grow to such an extent that Poland will have insufficient strength to cope with its neighbour to the East; as the Polish militarists recognise and openly acknowledge, time is working in the Soviet Union's favour. The Pilsudski press naturally comes to the conclusion that they need to embark on a preventive war, while the five-year plan is as yet uncompleted.

The Russians responded by stressing their own pacific intentions and repeating their longstanding offer of a non-aggression pact, supplemented by an expression of their readiness to "work for the intensification of economic and cultural relations" between the two countries. But these pleas fell on deaf ears. The Poles were too embroiled in a heated debate about the direction their foreign policy was now taking, to pay much attention to what they regarded as unwarranted hysteria in Moscow. The debate centred on the Polish Government's about-turn in policy towards Germany. This was anathema to the opposition National Democrats, prompting Roman Dmowski, a veteran statesman of the far Right not known for his love of the Soviet Union, to compose a series of articles claiming that the Government was planning to attack the Soviet Union.[41] Their publication only confirmed Moscow's worst fears:

> The threat of military adventures is so real that it forces the opponents of war with the Soviet Union in Poland to come forward at the present time with a warning against this highly dangerous policy...even in the Pilsudski camp there are individual elements coming out against war ... Roman Dmowski's two articles directly pointing to the preparation by Polish circles of an adventure in the East is an event the significance of which can not be overestimated. ... The fact that he ... has considered it necessary at the present moment to come forward with an exposure of the plans of Polish military circles, that the leader of the most Catholic of all Polish parties has been able to speak out openly against anti-Soviet adventures at a time when the Pope is organising a 'crusade', confirms the evaluation given by the Soviet press to the policy of the Polish 'colonels' ... Dmowski's statement is

too serious and too violent a means for this zealot of the Polish bourgeois state system ... to have recourse to, if it were not for the fact that the situation has become really serious.[42]

Further confirmation arrived on the very day this editorial appeared in *Izvestiya*. On the 11 April an article was published in *Gazeta Warszawska* entitled "Two Fronts". Arguing for the need to avoid the possibility of war on two fronts, it concluded that the weaker front — that facing the Soviet Union – should be liquidated first.[43] Russian alarm was unconcealed, but not until tension had reached its peak did the Polish Government finally decide to take these fears seriously. Foreign Minister Zaleski then announced to the world that no such war was being planned and that Poland sought peace. He admitted that improved relations with Germany had upset a third party, but also pointed to the fact that Poland was giving the Russians trade credits – hardly a sign of aggressive intentions. Referring to talks in Paris, he agreed that "may be there have been certain discussions about the dumping of Soviet products, but they were confined to considering commercial measures for meeting certain dangers ... Poland needs and wants peace".[44] However, this was insufficient to allay all Russian suspicions, particularly when, just over a week later, on the 26 April, a bomb was discovered in a central heating pipe at the Soviet embassy in Warsaw. The Russians always tended to view such incidents as attempts to provoke them into confict, a tendency accentuated by the tense state of relations between the two countries. Although the bomb appears to have been little more than an elaborate firework, the Soviet Government addressed a stern note to the Poles drawing their attention to the extreme dangers of the situation. The Poles apologised for the incident and took measures to punish those responsible. But the damage had been done. This was abundantly clear from the tone of a conversation between collegium member Stomonyakov and the Polish ambassador Patek on the 13 June. Patek's insistence on Poland's interest in peace rang hollow and prompted the bitter retort that "one comrade very well known to us [probably Stalin], in characterising the policy of the existing Polish Government towards the USSR, told me that it 'is attempting to keep the wound open'. This is very well said".[45]

The Soviet Union's problems with Poland and Germany were

only partly offset by the welcome and timely improvement in Anglo-Soviet relations signalled by the signature of a temporary trade agreement on the 16 April.[46] Negotiations on that subject had dragged on since the restoration of diplomatic contacts and had threatened to flounder in a new wave of anti-Sovietism sweeping across Britain. On the day after signature, *Izvestiya* hailed the agreement as an event of primary importance. The "political significance of this agreement goes beyond the limits of Anglo-Soviet trade and Anglo-Soviet relations", an editorial noted, adding that it was *"impossible not to consider it a fact facilitating the cause of peace and foiling the militaristic plans of world reaction"*.[47] Not surprisingly foreign observers noted a visible easing of anxiety amongst Soviet officialdom.[48] However, the impact of this coup was significantly reduced by two counter-veiling factors. Firstly, it left the roots of tension in relations untouched, and, secondly, Britain was by now being displaced by France as the dominant Power in Europe. Unfortunately for the Russians, the most immediate cause of continuing British hostility towards the Bolsheviks – Moscow's aid to national liberation movements in Asia – was shortly to join a mounting list of grievances directed against the USSR by the French Government.

Britain had made no progress at all in obtaining a genuine commitment from the Soviet authorities to desist from using the Comintern to sponsor revolutionary agitation throughout the British empire, particularly in India.[49] It was evidently this that prompted British aid to the Basmachi rebels operating from bases in Northern Afghanistan against Soviet Central Asia. The British Government was now retaliating in kind. Throughout the twenties there had been a certain amount of friction between Moscow and Kabul due to banditry on the part of Basmachi tribesmen. By the end of the decade, however, the Russians appeared to have solved the problem.[50] In addition a raid by the Red Army across the Oxus failed to elicit any promise of aid to Kabul from London in the event of a full-scale Soviet assault on the country.[51] This resulted in a shift of influence to the advantage of the Russians. Not until 1929, with the outbreak of civil war in Afghanistan, was Britain able to recover lost ground. Given the ephemeral basis for Soviet influence in Kabul – subsidies to a regime no longer able to rule[52] – London soon regained the initiative. When King Nadir Shah came victoriously to the throne in November 1929, the British made "veiled attempts" to induce him into accepting a subsidy to stabilise the new regime,[53] and by February 1930 Voroshilov was publicly voicing Soviet anxiety at the strengthening of British influence in Afghanistan.[54] The significance of this transcended diplomacy. The collectivisation of agriculture in Soviet Central Asia was meeting with growing resistance from the local population, leading to a resurgence in Basmachi revolts, particularly in Tadzhikistan. The Russian press stressed the role of "English agents", who were said to be "activating Basmachi aggressiveness against Soviet Central Asia".[55] These claims were not without foundation. Apparently British interest in the Basmachi was awakened in the autumn of 1929 with the attempts by Ibrahim Beg to unite them under one banner. The British military attaché in Meshed, Major Steveni, brought the various factions together for talks in order to facilitate this process.[56] Conditions were ripe for revolt and not only in Soviet Central Asia. In March 1930 there were reports of "serious anti-governmental disturbances" from Baku in the Caucasus to Ganjah and Daghestan.[57] Some 1200 Turkomans in the Merv-Tejend district opposed to collectivisation had moved into the Karakum area. Two punitive expeditions were reportedly sent in to deal with them, but both were forced to retreat after suffering heavy losses at the hands of the Turkomans.[58] By the beginning of April reports of Basmachi activity in the Samarkand region were also reaching Steveni in Meshed.[59] Furthermore, the tension which arose in Soviet-Afghan relations as a result of Basmachi operations from Northern Afghanistan created ideal conditions for British diplomacy in Kabul. The Afghans, formerly hesitant about offers of aid from the British, now informed them that a subsidy was acceptable, in the form of arms and money and in return for friendship with London.[60] The ousting of Soviet influence from Kabul in June 1930 therefore left the Russians only too aware that their progress in relations with Britain was severely constrained by the continuation of fierce rivalry beyond the frontiers of Europe, and that their domestic problems had presented a golden opportunity for exploitation by the capitalist world.

Whereas relations between Moscow and London had long been strained by Soviet aid to national liberation movements in the East, this had always played a lesser role where Franco-Soviet relations were concerned. France, of course, possessed a more modest empire, with less scope for Comintern activity, though it was merely an accident of fate that no revolt of any significance had occurred there in the postwar period. But there was also never any doubt that in the event of unrest the Comintern would step in with both moral and, where possible, material support. Such decisions appear to have been made without any consideration as to the diplomatic repercussions that would inevitably ensue. It was still a fixed belief within the Soviet Communist Party that in the long-term much would depend upon the success of the revolution elsewhere in the world, and although Stalin was sceptical of the chances of success, he none the less appears to have been loath to interfere with Comintern activities except in extreme emergencies. This was certainly the case in 1930 with respect to relations with France and the rebellion in Indochina.

On the 25 March French Foreign Minister Briand had disingenuously described the Kutepov affair as merely "an incident, a sensation, which could not seriously damage Franco-Soviet relations".[61] But this was because by then another issue had arisen which did threaten to do so: Comintern involvement in the revolt which had just broken out in French Indochina. Never entirely quiescent under French rule, the territory had seen revolts on a significant scale with unerring regularity from 1885 to 1912. Then followed a period of relative tranquillity until the depression in world prices for raw materials severely hit the country's exports and the economy as a whole. The price of rice, for example, fell by 50 per cent; of maize by 75 per cent, quite apart from minerals such as tin (54 per cent), lead (50 per cent), zinc (45 per cent) and materials such as rubber (65 per cent) and coal (14 per cent). Combined with a highly inequitable distribution of land and an immiserated workforce, this provided conditions ripe for revolt.

During the night of the 9 to the 10 February 1930 two companies from the fourth regiment of the tirailleurs Tonkinois, accompanied by sixty or so local revolutionaries, attacked the garrison at Yen-Bay, some 160 kilometres from Hanoi. Although order was soon re-established and casualties were slight, similar outbursts elsewhere and subsequent interrogations of those arrested made it clear that this was an uprising "carried out on the instructions of the leaders of the Viet-Nam in China" (the nationalists).[62] But it was not long before a Communist presence made itself felt. Two telegrams reached Paris in quick succession. The first, from Herbette in Moscow, dated the 20 February, passed on information "from a serious foreign source" that "numerous revolutionary propagandists have recently been sent from here to Indochina via Vladivostok and Chinese ports such as Shanghai".[63] On the following day, the French Governor-General, Pasquier, sent a message from Hanoi with news that a Communist government had been set up in Long Tchéou several days previously "by agitators from Shanghai".[64]

The Catholic mission had been burnt down and the French consulate sacked, and its codes captured by the local soviet.[65] Up to now Communist activity had posed no real problem to the authorities. As Pasquier noted: "Soviet propaganda had not been able to operate except amongst a highly restricted circle of malcontents, and the vast majority of the population scarcely knew of its existence".[66] Lack of unity (by autumn 1929 there were three separate Communist groupings as a result of the failure to agree on the foundation of a party in May), discord with the Viet-Nam (a by-product of the split between the Kuomintang and the Communists in China) and the absence of links with the Comintern, all contributed to this relative impotence.[67] By the end of 1929, however, the Sûreté had uncovered Communist munition dumps in Hadong and Bac Ninh, and, although Pasquier was reluctant to admit it, this discovery augured badly for the future.[68] The Comintern was making up for lost time. In October 1929 its leadership had decided on the unification of the three groupings into a single Communist Party (Cong San Dang), accomplished at a special congress in Hong Kong on the 3 February 1930, barely a week before the events at Yen-Bay.[69]

It is curious that in Moscow no regard for the effects of Comintern agitation on relations with France was apparently allowed to hamper the progress of the revolution in Indochina. Two irreconcilable objectives – peaceful co-existence and class warfare – were being pursued by different arms of the same authority, and at a time when circumstances dictated the need for settled relations with the Powers. Clearly the left hand was not exactly unaware of, but was certainly unresponsive to, what the right hand was attempting to do, whilst Stalin, preoccupied as ever with the twists and turns of domestic politics, typically felt disinclined to intervene on one side or the other.

Whilst Briand remonstrated with Dovgalevsky about Soviet involvement,[70] the Far Eastern section of the Comintern took charge of the Communist movement in Indochina,[71] where slogans for May Day tactlessly included the call for union with Soviet Russia.[72] And as the Communists grew more successful, the temperature in Paris rose accordingly. In mid-May Pasquier informed his masters that: "As a result of an undeniable tenacity, anti-French propaganda has more or less been completely unified under the . . . guiding hand of the Cong San".[73] The Colonial Minister, Piétri, then addressed the Chamber of Deputies on the subject. There, on the 13 June, he described the troubles in Tonkin as "the realisation of a long and detailed plot". They shared a characteristic with the uprisings further south, in their "vigilant exploitation . . . by the leaders of Communism". He went on to describe the sequence of events in lurid and melodramatic terms:

> It is clear – and it has been necessary to say so here, without deviation – that the action of Bolshevik Communism, led and paid for by the permanent agency which the propagators of the Third International maintain in Canton, has systematically aimed at and threatened France's position in Indochina, and that a plot, prepared down to the last detail and merely interrupted by the measures taken in 1929, had as its goal the complete destruction of our rule.

Not surprisingly, this imaginative account precipitated calls for the removal of the Soviet embassy from French soil. Encouraged, the Minister then incautiously suggested that, should the idea of a common defence of the colonies against propaganda be raised at the League of Nations, he would take an active part in the matter. But this merely whetted the appetite of other deputies, who called on him to take the initiative. However, he had evidently gone as far as, if not further than, his colleagues would permit; he therefore evaded the suggestion entirely.[74]

In the event, despite the considerable extent of the revolt,[75] a mixture of timely reforms and brutal repression – the leading nationalist Nguyen Thai Hoc was executed, and Tran Phu, the general secretary of the Cong San was arrested and so badly tortured that he died the following year[76] – saw the colony firmly restored to French rule. Interestingly, although the revolt stirred up enormous hostility against the USSR in France, it led to no direct and concrete reprisals by the French authorities. Clearly enmity towards the Soviet Union was merely fuelled by events such as the Kutepov affair and the Indochinese revolt. The underlying causes appear to have lain deeper, for the anti-Soviet campaign in France now shifted its focus to the crisis in commercial relations with Moscow.

4 The USSR Faces a Campaign against Dumping

By flooding a depressed world market with raw materials and agricultural produce in order to support the foreign exchange burden of the five-year plan, the Russians came into direct collision with powerful industrial and agrarian lobbies, West and East. For although France took the lead in combatting Soviet dumping, it was also an issue which complicated Moscow's relations with almost every Power and fast became the main element in destabilising the USSR's hard-won peaceful co-existence with the capitalist world.

The first battle the Russians faced was with the Americans. The only Great Power that consistently refused to grant official recognition to the Soviet regime, the USA had nevertheless become its third largest trading partner by 1929.[1] This was only partly due to the pervasive admiration for American products – *amerikanomaniya* – it was also a means by which the Soviet Government hoped to win recognition. But it proved a double-edged sword. Why recognise the USSR diplomatically – no advantage in itself – when there was no economic incentive to do so? As the Russians were soon forced to admit: "the opponents of recognition have zealously used the fact that Soviet orders have grown as evidence that even without recognition trade with the USSR is possible"; the inescapable conclusion being that "despite the expansion of our business relations with America . . . we see no alteration from the hostile position which America adopts in relation to us; more than that, we have not even obtained security from administrative measures in relation to our exports".[2] The anti-dumping lobby had begun to make itself felt early in 1930 when, as a result of pressure from the Pennsylvania coal industry, Washington took steps to investigate the possibility of taking measures to restrict Soviet sales.[3] The lumber industry was more successful, for on the 25 July the administration announced a ban on imports of timber from the USSR. The Russians were swift to react. Three days later Peter Bogdanov, the chairman of Amtorg (a Soviet-owned joint stock company handling trade with the USA), issued a statement to the press warning that "cutting the importation of Soviet goods into the USA will assuredly affect its [the USSR's] purchases in this country".[4] Forced to reconsider, the administration then grudgingly raised the ban on the 2 August. Having won, *Pravda* then demanded "Complete Clarity", taking Bogdanov's threats one step further: "Are normal trade relations conceivable in an atmosphere of vagueness and uncertainty, created by anti-Soviet campaigns?".[5] One important reason why the Americans lost the battle was that they had acted alone, and at this stage the Russians had little reason to believe that circumstances would alter: "competition between capitalist states opens up for the Soviet Union the possibility of distributing its orders to places where a more normal basis for their realisation exists".[6] But as summer turned to autumn a chill wind began to cool even the most ardent optimist.

Neither Britain (via the Dominions) nor Italy were yet substantially affected by Soviet dumping, and Germany remained one of the few countries to be left entirely undisturbed. Elsewhere, however, general action to insulate essentially agrarian economies from the impact of the Depression was soon coloured by anti-Soviet sentiment. Beginning in June 1930 with a meeting of the Little Entente (Romania, Czechoslovakia and Yugoslavia) – as much concerned at US tariffs as Soviet dumping – a series of conferences ensued, involving a growing number of East European states; this included a meeting in Warsaw at the end of August, to which the Russians alone were not invited, where the Romanians proposed the formation of an agrarian bloc stretching from the Baltic to the Black Sea.[7] Any close co-operation between the participants (Belgium, Estonia, Hungary, Latvia, Poland, Romania, Czechoslovakia and Yugoslavia) was unwelcome to the Russians, particularly as they suspected that behind this facade lurked the machinations of the Great Powers, especially France. On the 28 August, the day the conference opened, *Pravda* facetiously though nonetheless apprehensively suggested that "evidently the main 'agrarian advisers' will be

officers from the French general staff".[8] Certainly Polish Foreign
Minister Zaleski's attempt, in his opening speech, to link the work
of the conference to the Briand plan for a federated Europe (see
below) did nothing to lessen such fears. As one Soviet
commentator remarked, the initiators of the conference were only
"formally" the agrarian and agrarian-industrialised countries.
"But in reality behind this 'green' blockade stand the financial
sharks of world imperialism and the organisers of an anti-Soviet
war".[9] If any doubts remained, the grounds that the Lithuanian
Foreign Minister Dr Zaunius gave for not participating in the next
conference (held at Bucharest in October) – that "political
tendencies were likely to prevail" with "the formation of a bloc
embracing both the Black and Baltic Seas" – appeared proof
enough that some dark design was afoot.[10]

What was so disturbing to the Russians was France's likely
presence behind the scenes. For although relations between
Moscow and Paris miraculously survived both the Kutepov affair
and the revolt in Indochina, the whole direction of French policy
was seen as inimical to Soviet interests. The Russians were long
haunted by the apparition of a united Europe, and in May
1930, with international enmity towards the USSR still at an
uncomfortable pitch, Briand put forward his ideas for a
European federation in a memorandum circulated to the Powers.
Its distinguishing feature was its nebulousness, with bland
references to the need for solidarity among "European
Governments" in the organisation of "European peace" and the
rational management of the continent's "vital forces".[11] The
Russians nonetheless eyed it with extreme suspicion. "For us any,
even a partial, stabilisation of capitalist states is dangerous,
especially if it is accomplished under France's leadership", wrote
the polpred in Vienna, Yurenev, in another context.[12] Thus
Soviet missions throughout Europe were instructed to stress
Moscow's negative attitude towards the proposals and the harm
they could do to states excluded from the projected federation.[13]
But Litvinov was a realist par excellence and was well aware that
Soviet attempts to sabotage the proposals might fail. He therefore
trod warily, avoiding a direct confrontation with the French in
the hope of securing an invitation to the forthcoming discussions at
Geneva – true to his philosophy of joining any gathering which
might become a forum for anti-Soviet activities. Thus, when faced
with Herbette in late July 1930, he "strongly denied the rumour

according to which the Government of the USSR had sent a circular to other states concerning the French memorandum", which was, strictly speaking, true, though more than a little misleading; and it is worth noting that this sentence does not appear in Litvinov's account of the conversation.[14]

Meanwhile, trade relations between the two countries were rapidly disintegrating for quite different reasons, though the atmosphere of mistrust engendered by the crisis in political relations undoubtedly had its influence on events here as well. Commerce between France and the USSR had never amounted to much, for the French had early reacted to the Soviet refusal to honour pre-revolutionary debts by directly discouraging trade. A government decree published in the *Journal Officiel* on the 6 December 1920 declined "all responsibility with regard to transactions undertaken by traders or industrialists, who are acting entirely at their own risk". It was thus logical for the French Government to refuse to guarantee credits for Soviet purchases, in contrast to both Germany and Britain. Not surprisingly, therefore, this was reflected in the low level of trade. In 1929 France took only 4.1 per cent of the USSR's total trade, as against Germany's massive 22.7 per cent, Britain's 14.3 per cent (not yet recovered from the breach in 1927) and the USA's respectable 12.1 per cent. Furthermore, in 1930 the French share fell to 3.5 per cent and within this reduced figure Soviet exports to France actually rose, whereas French sales to the USSR dropped.[15] When the French complained at their diminishing market in the USSR, Soviet representatives replied by insisting that government-backed credits were vital for Moscow to finance further orders from France.[16] Soviet indifference was reinforced by the absence of a trade agreement between the two countries providing the Soviet trade mission in Paris with legal status and therefore immunity to indemnification for losses suffered by creditors to pre-Bolshevik Russia. This became a vital issue in the spring of 1930.

Hertzfeld, one of those who had, as a result of Soviet policy, lost money in Russia, took his claims to a French court, which found in his favour and ordered the seizure of Soviet assets in France on the 5 March 1930. This decision spelt calamity not merely for Soviet companies operating there, but also for the fate of the trade mission itself. In response, Litvinov pointedly remarked at a public gathering that "commercial activity between the two countries is on the verge of passing away because it lacks a legal basis".[17] But the Russians had not given up all hope. An editorial in the Narkomindel's German-language paper, *Moskauer Rundschau*, argued that the French had never responded to proposals made in September 1927 for a settlement of certain debts in return for making credit available,[18] and stressed the need to normalise trade relations.[19] The Russians also took legal action, appealing to a higher authority against the original decision, but the appeal court suspended judgement on the substance of the matter, whilst simultaneously confirming the seizure (24 July).[20] The harder edge to Soviet attitudes now broke through. Two days later, Litvinov informed Herbette that the Soviet trade mission had been instructed to make no payments and satisfy no creditors for whom the Soviets had no direct responsibility, even if a seizure was effected. Herbette was further told that the building occupied by the mission had been sold and that instructions had been sent to refrain from making any deposit in French banks. "It is the very existence of our trade mission which is at stake", Litvinov warned.[21] However, even when Hertzfeld began to effect the seizure of goods belonging to various Soviet organisations in France the Russians, whilst issuing ominous warnings,[22] continued to leave the door open for negotiations.[23] In the meantime Soviet exporters redirected their products to Hamburg, whence they were transported to France by rail under the label of a French company to mislead the French customs.[24]

In Paris they were uncertain which course to take. The choice was whether to climb down and open negotiations, as the Russians clearly desired, or, on the contrary, move onto the offensive. Initially the tendency was to seek a compromise which would increase the volume of trade with Moscow. On the 8 August Flandin, Minister of Commerce and Industry, wrote to Briand with proposals for finding credits for the USSR from a source other than the Banque de France.[25] Evidently taking the cue, the European section at the Quai d'Orsay stressed the need to negotiate with the Russians before the government was compelled to surrender to them under pressure from public opinion. But other factors, of a more general political nature, were behind these proposals: "the conclusion of an economic and financial agreement with the USSR would diminish the impact of a German–Soviet–Italian entente for the revision of the treaties".[26] However, these considerations were left to gather dust on the shelves of the Quai d'Orsay, in the absence of any compelling and urgent need to prise the Russians apart from the Germans and the Italians, and in the face of ideological objections which overshadowed any sense of realpolitik. For Briand dismissed out of hand any notion of compromise with the Russians,[27] and in an atmosphere already poisoned against the Soviet Union, agricultural interests successfully lobbied for action against Soviet dumping in France.[28] The Ministry of Agriculture's proposed solution to this problem provided the French Government with an alternative strategy for dealing with the Russians without having to offer them anything in return. This policy "would favour the establishment of an anti-dumping organisation as well as being an action leading to an improvement in the balance of our exchanges with the Soviets".[29] It was with this in mind that Elbel, a top official in Flandin's ministry, was despatched to Geneva with instructions to sound out other governments on joint action in this field, as a result of which the second commission of the League assembly was asked to consider a proposal for establishing an entente to combat Soviet dumping.[30]

The French Government did not wait until its attempts to coordinate action with other countries had succeeded. On the 3 October the Ministry of Commerce and Industry introduced restrictions on imports from the Soviet Union. The decree came at a most unfortunate moment, which led to a serious misunderstanding in Moscow over the true meaning of this act. For only the previous day Herbette, preoccupied with Nazi successes at the September elections, had broached the idea of a Franco-Soviet non-aggression pact in an amicable conversation with Litvinov.[31] The Russians therefore initially took the decree less seriously than otherwise they might have done. *Izvestiya* thus carried an editorial on the 5 October entitled "The French Adventure", which suggested that "the current anti-Soviet outburst of the French Government has been dictated by the wish to demonstrate that France's wings have still not been clipped" and continued with the assertion that the decree was designed for domestic effect, the USSR being made the scapegoat for France's economic difficulties. It was "a direct manifestation of panic", a "sign of weakness". On sober reflection, however, and as the French renewed their attempts to universalise their approach to Soviet dumping, the Russians showed increasing concern. The memorandum formulated by Dovgalevsky in the light of instructions from Moscow and handed to the French over a week later, pointed to a real danger that the decree could be "construed as a first step on the road to the achievement of a programme of general economic activities against the USSR".[32] Indeed, this prognosis was not wide of the mark. Not only did Berthelot, the Quai d'Orsay's general secretary, "show not the slightest interest in finding a way out of the situation",[33] but other countries were following suit (notably Belgium[34] and Hungary) as a result of pressure from Paris. Flandin, now nicknamed "the Minister for Dumping" by the Russians,[35] toured Eastern Europe to gather support, and despite strenuous denials from the Quai that he was attempting "to organise concerted economic action against the USSR",[36] his activities in Budapest and Prague – where he asked the Czechs to consider an embargo on imports from the USSR[37] – belied these assurances.

The Soviet reaction was one of blustering defiance, typified in a *Pravda* editorial on the 20 October, two days after the opening of the Bucharest conference where East European states were deciding what action to take (with little result), and on the very day the Russians launched a counter-offensive by prohibiting all imports from France:

> Whipping up a frenzied campaign about alleged "Soviet dumping", and making use of the most severe crisis that has hit the Baltic and Balkan states, French imperialism is carrying out its aggressive programme for the preparation of a new intervention against the USSR. French imperialism is *counting on* the Soviet Union's Western neighbours and their closest "allies". However, the heroic struggle of the peasant masses against the yoke of Polish Fascism in the Western Ukraine, the insurrectionary movement in Romania and Bessarabia and, finally, the exacerbation of economic and political contradictions in France itself, making its working masses increasingly revolutionary – all this shows that French imperialism's calculations will come to nought.[38]

To a great extent the Russians were whistling in the dark,

but their retaliation certainly threw the French into considerable confusion. Not having sufficiently thought through the
implications of their action, they now found themselves in an
impasse. The mercurial Herbette suffered a sudden attack of
nerves and, two days after the appearance of the Soviet decree,
counselled Paris to offer the Russians long-term credits at low
cost, in order to undermine Soviet determination to persist in
their retaliation![39] In the French capital, Dovgalevsky was as
optimistic as his counterpart was pessimistic, and was easily taken
in by words of sympathy from some in high places, which he took
to mean not merely divisions within the conseil d'état, but also
favourable prospects for negotiations.[40] However, in Moscow
Krestinsky was far less hopeful, seeing such disclosures as part of a
premeditated move to distract the Russians from manoeuvring
against the French at Geneva, "a ruse quite typical of French
diplomacy",[41] and although he tended to overplay the
perfidiousness of the French, his lack of optimism was to prove
justified. For, if Paris was still listening to its embassy in Moscow,
then the diehards received further encouragement from Herbette
who, having recovered from his initial agitation, was now swayed
by an "English expert" recently arrived in the Soviet capital. He
informed Briand that the Soviet Union was, in fact, in a
precarious financial position: "it is in no condition to intimidate
anybody", he wrote, adding that "we therefore have no reason for
being discouraged or for taking hasty action".[42] With this, both
France and the Soviet Union appeared to be drifting irrevocably
towards a breach in relations and, as the Russians always feared,
the possibility of something even worse.

5 Attempts to Counter the Threat from France

Economic sanctions by France predetermined the whole course of Soviet foreign policy from their introduction in the autumn of 1930. Even after their withdrawal was negotiated in the spring of 1931, the importance Moscow then attached to the signature of a non-aggression pact with France proved "curiously illustrative of the lingering suspicion of foreign military intervention".[1] This saw its domestic reflection in the trial of the so-called 'Industrial Party' in November 1930, where absurd plots involving the French first and foremost were put on display to warn the Soviet public of the war danger. Indeed, the French obsession cast such a shadow that the combined forces of Soviet diplomacy, foreign trade and Comintern activities were mobilised to neutralise the threats from France, both real and imaginary.

Given the continuing Soviet boycott of the League of Nations, the most convenient international forum for conducting a diplomatic counter-offensive against the French was the preparatory commission on disarmament at Geneva. The Russians, like many others, were in favour of disarmament in principle, but were none the less in two minds as to whether participation at Geneva was useful or counter-productive. When in April 1929 the French Government persuaded the commission to shelve disarmament as a first priority in favour of "security", the Soviets withdrew from the proceedings in order to avoid lending further credence to a bankrupt enterprise.[2] But with Litvinov firmly ensconced at the head of the Narkomindel, the Soviet Government relented. Litvinov considered that the USSR's absence from international conferences merely facilitated concerted action against Soviet interests. He was always conscious of the need to use any platform to enhance the USSR's image as a country devoted to world peace. These views were spelt out at the press conference following his appointment as Commissar in July 1930:

46

We will readily support undertakings and proposals aimed at making military conflict impossible and safeguarding peace in general. We will, however, take on the role of merciless prosecutors in those cases where we can see that the hypocritical mask of pacifist phraseology hides desires and interests which have nothing in common with peace and with the real interests of the people. We will limit our role to that of observers in those cases where the real aims of international gestures are insufficiently clear to us and need precise definition and exposure.[3]

The implementation of economic sanctions by France then made vital a return to Geneva for, as *Izvestiya* noted, the talks on disarmament were "*a method of struggle amongst the imperialists*",[4] and, although this could not be said publicly, they were also a means the Russians could successfully exploit in their struggle with the French. So when the commission finally reconvened on the 6 November Litvinov launched his assault. "The fact must be recognised", he declared, "that the thesis of 'security' at the present time and in the manner defended by its supporters is directed against disarmament, and that the defenders of this doctrine are at present working against disarmament and against even a reduction in armaments". In contrast, Litvinov presented the Soviet position as both positive and realistic. "We believe", he asserted, ". . . otherwise we would not be here – that the danger of war can significantly be reduced or postponed for a time by means of certain real disarmament measures."[5] A week later the Soviet delegation duly put forward its own proposals.[6] But they made no headway. On the contrary, the commission now accepted a convention defining the agenda for the forthcoming disarmament conference, which pessimistically spoke of reducing armaments "as far as possible". The convention included within it caveats which threatened to make any disarmament measures worthless. In an effort to appease France and its allies, the commission had accepted article 50 which allowed states that felt threatened to infringe the limitations imposed by the convention. Litvinov therefore dissociated the Soviet Government from the whole affair, giving a press conference in which he made public Soviet objections.[7]

Rejection of the commission's work did not mean withdrawal from Geneva. Ever mindful of the dangers of isolation in the face of continuing French intrigues, Litvinov was also careful to announce that a Soviet delegation would nonetheless attend the forthcoming disarmament conference as part of the USSR's "tireless struggle for peace".[8] In private he told Grandi that although he did not believe anything concrete would result from the conference, it nevertheless provided "a means which, if ably exploited by us, could create considerable trouble for France and her allies". This also explained Litvinov's interest in securing an invitation to participate in the commission on the Briand plan; however, in Moscow opinion on that matter was still divided.[9]

In any struggle with France, Italy was a natural ally. Grandi spoke of the Briand proposals as part of "the plan for European hegemony" which the French were unfolding for the third time this century.[10] Furthermore, there were apparently no obstacles to close co-operation between the USSR and a Fascist Power. On the contrary, of all the capitalist countries, relations with Italy had hitherto proved the least complicated, despite the irreconcilability of Fascism with Communism. The spirit of pragmatism that prevailed was well summed up and defended by Grandi in a speech to the Gran Consiglio, on the 2 October 1930:

The ideology of a political party is in reality one thing, the action of a government is another. The former moves in the absolute, the latter amidst real facts, practical possibilities, duties and responsibilities more vast and likewise more determinant for the defence and protection of not only the immediate, but above all the distant and future interests of the Nation ... What someone chose to call the *new* policy of Italy towards Soviet Russia is not, however, a novelty. One of the first accomplishments of Mussolini's foreign policy on the morrow of the March on Rome was precisely the Italo-Soviet commercial agreement of 1923 and the institution of normal diplomatic relations between Rome and Moscow.

Fascist Italy was the first European nation to enter into normal relations with Russia,[11] and this was done even whilst the smoke was still rising from the ruins of the Communist organisation which Fascism destroyed. The latter was an act of courage and supreme wisdom which showed that Italy did not then intend, as it does not intend today, to subordinate the permanent interests of the Nation to the interests of a political ideology. Fascism is not — as Mussolini has said and reiterated — an article for export, neither was it ever meant to be a universal idea or even an ideology; it is simply a way of life for Italy, it is meant to be the synthesis of our historical experience and of the aspirations and particular national needs of our people and our race.[12]

This was a language Litvinov and Stalin understood; in fact, Soviet diplomats were fond of citing relations with Rome as eloquent testimony of their total indifference to the internal affairs of other states.[13] The Italian Communist Party was thus left to its fate. The Great Depression may have increased its support as an underground movement, but an attempt to return its operational headquarters to Italy proved a dreadful failure. The Party amounted to only a few thousand members and Mussolini's political police soon ensured that any advances made were shortlived.[14]

Although the fact that Grandi had to defend his realpolitik to the Gran Consiglio showed that the Italians were not entirely as pragmatic as the Russians about the direction of their diplomacy, they were nonetheless sufficiently disturbed by the Briand plan to seek Soviet participation at the forthcoming talks on the subject. They informed the Narkomindel of this early in July 1930.[15] Events then reinforced Moscow's interest in co-operation. On the 3 September a "high official" of the Revvoensovet (Revolutionary Military Council) pressed Persico, the Italian chargé d'affaires, for joint moves to counter French intrigues in Turkey, adding hopefully that "Italy and the USSR are unique amongst the nations of Europe in that not only are they not divided by any dispute, but on the contrary, they have interests in common."[16] At the same time, in fact on that very day, the concern expressed by Herbette at rumours of "a far-reaching rapprochement between the USSR and Italy"[17] came as a welcome reminder to the Russians that ties with Rome could prove extremely valuable as a means of striking back at the French.

Litvinov was naturally eager to formalise any rapprochement with the signature of a non-aggression pact, which he and his superiors appeared to regard as the ultimate litmus test in world politics. Although he himself did not believe that the Soviet Union now faced the prospect of war, "many of his colleagues in the government" were "preoccupied with being attacked militarily by the capitalist states any day".[18] It was evidently this that prompted Litvinov to seek a meeting with Grandi, which was held in Milan on the 24 November. There he "confirmed ... his desire that *'something be done'* formally between the two countries which would give public expression" to Italo-Soviet cordiality.[19] But both men had built up too many expectations. For his part Litvinov unfortunately found Grandi more reticent on the issue of a pact than he had hoped. This was not surprising. Grandi's superiors were most reluctant to sanction too overt a flirtation with Bolshevik Russia. It might alienate the other Powers, rather than merely provoke them into a recognition of Italy's importance. The Italian Foreign Ministry were therefore obliged, as well as mostly pleased, to work on the assumption that the Soviet Union was merely a "card" to be held "in reserve" and was not to be used "as a bogey against the other players".[20]

Undeterred and irrepressible, Litvinov continued to explore every avenue. On returning to Moscow at the end of November, he immediately contacted the Italian embassy and, as Persico reported:

> He put to me ... his own ideas about the general situation, dominated, as he sees it, by France, whose privileges derived from treaties, the power she possesses in terms of armaments and financial prosperity, the network of politico-military alliances she has with a series of vassal states, assure her a growing and menacing hegemony which, as such, cannot be viewed with anything other than anxiety by other countries.
>
> Hence the need for an entente between our countries, not in the form of an alliance, which the Soviets are against as a matter of principle, but a natural cohesion manifesting itself in closer collaboration and in coordinated and concrete action.[21]

This was more than one step further than a non-aggression pact, and at the outset it looked as though Grandi was most unlikely to take up such a suggestion. For he, too, was offered less than expected at Milan. The Italians had hoped to secure a definite commitment from the Russians to accept a place on the League commission set up to deal with the Briand plan. Litvinov, however, was forced to confess that no such undertaking could yet be given because opinion on participation was still divided in Moscow.[22] Thus, as Grandi explained later to Mussolini: "After the meeting with Litvinov at Milan and after our ambassador in Moscow confirmed that the Russian Government was uncertain at the prospect of Russia's participation in the European commission, I had decided, prior to my departure for Geneva, not to go too far in committing Italy on this question."[23] But, faced once again with "the infallibility of Pope Briand" in the "sacred precincts of Geneva",[24] he was immediately reminded of Russia's continuing value. The issue of Russian, and indeed Turkish, participation in the European commission presented him with "a field for manoeuvre"[25] against France, "the landlord and banker of Europe".[26]

At Geneva "the admission of Bolshevik Russia requested by Fascist Italy constituted an almost insuperable psychological obstacle for many".[27] It was therefore no surprise that Grandi, with less than full support from the more cautious German delegation, was only partly successful; and even then much of this was attributable to the British wish for compromise.[28] Although admitted, the Russians were not permitted to participate in discussions on anything other than economic issues – a "semi-victory" as Krestinsky termed it.[29] There was clearly a danger that this snub to Russian pride might reinforce existing objections to appearing at Geneva. But Litvinov's pragmatism prevailed. Although a shadow of dissent could be seen in the wordy Soviet note accepting the League invitation,[30] Litvinov's preferred tactics were now grudgingly accepted as official policy. "Despite the ambiguities in the invitation delivered to the Soviet Union to participate in the special conference of the European commission", Molotov told the sixth congress of Soviets, "the Soviet Government considered it necessary to accept, so that it can ascertain on the spot what the plans and aims of this organisation are".[31] A half-hearted invitation had elicited a less than full-hearted response, but Litvinov could now exploit the opportunity for all it was worth.

More than a trace of bitterness was evident in the biting sarcasm with which Litvinov delivered his opening speech to the European commission on the 18 May. "Mr Chairman," he declared: "allow me first to express to you my gratitude for the extremely kind words of welcome addressed to those newly arrived in Europe. The fact of my presence here will certainly inspire great joy in the hearts of all geographers of the world, since this will, if only partly, confirm the hypothesis that the territory of the former Russian empire is still situated in Europe." Yet the bulk of his speech was nevertheless conciliatory. After arguing, on the one hand, that the Soviet Union was quite different from the rest of the world in its economic growth, he then proceeded to claim its identity with other countries in export practices. With this necessary piece of special pleading, he went on to stress the interdependence of Soviet economic expansion and the development of world trade.[32] Finally, he unveiled his *pièce de résistance* – a draft pact of economic non-aggression, designed to prevent the very measures which France had introduced during the previous autumn.[33] But there was no sign that this proposal would meet with general or even partial acceptance. The spirit of protectionism hung like a pall over the proceedings at Geneva, and the Great Powers spent more time coping with the recently announced Austro-German customs union – discussed on p.63 below – than in dealing with the larger issues relating to Europe's overall economic and political condition. Nonetheless the Russians had lost nothing by their appearance at the League and had arguably gained much from the attendant publicity. Litvinov himself felt that it pointed to "a significant mollification in relations with Western Europe", successfully extending the "breathing-space" needed for the accomplishment of the five-year plan.[34] This view was not only shared in Moscow,[35] it also gave added impetus to the Commissar's peace policy. Instructions accordingly went out to all diplomatic missions abroad "to 'play up' M. Litvinov's suggestions at Geneva" and, as the British ambassador noted, "every Russian official with whom one talks makes some reference to the principle of co-existence of countries, irrespective of their social-political and economic systems'". In the words of Lunacharsky, a close friend of the Commissar, all this was due "to the personal initiative of M. Litvinov".[36] The occasion therefore marked something of a turning-point in Soviet diplomacy, though what was successfully accomplished at Geneva was symbolic rather than solid. The Russians still waited on the whims of the other Powers; they were not yet strong enough to stand alone, and even the most friendly amongst the Western states were far from reliable as allies.

In this respect, too much should not be read into the Italian Government's sponsorship of the USSR at Geneva; it was merely a tactic temporarily useful in manoeuvres against France. The Italians saw no long-term interest in the enhancement of Soviet power. This was clearly enunciated in a letter from Grandi to

Attolico dated the 21 March 1931. Although "our policy must be directed towards maintaining good relations with Soviet Russia", he wrote, it could not "venture so far as to offer excessive help in consolidating the Soviet Government by facilitating its ability to overcome difficulties and uncertainties in its foreign policy, the very continuation of which might be turned to our advantage".[37] One could scarcely find a more unambiguous sign that Moscow still stood uncertainly on the periphery of European politics than this comment from a Great Power of the second rank. A visible indication of this was Italy's willingness to participate in a treaty limiting naval armaments, the bases for which were agreed with France and Britain on the 1 March.[38] Designed partly to show "that Italy ... does not intend to disturb world peace",[39] it came as a bitter blow to the Russians. Ever-anxious to keep the Western Powers at odds with one another and over-optimistic at the prospects for Italo-Soviet co-operation against France, the Russians despondently referred to it as "a victory for French imperialism".[40]

*   *   *

The diplomatic game thus often produced insubstantial results. The Russians were wise to direct their efforts towards the expansion of foreign trade for political purposes. The sum total of their trade was, of course, a product of economic necessity. But its distribution was easily shaped by political considerations without any great economic loss incurred. The Russians could afford to select their imports from a wide variety of shrinking markets desperate for business. The state monopoly of foreign trade, so zealously defended since Lenin, now proved of inestimable value politically. Trade could be mobilised as a direct instrument of foreign policy. Although not entirely new, the massive scale of the trade serving the USSR's industrialisation programme, when combined with the devastating collapse in demand within the capitalist world, now made it a hefty weight on the diplomatic scales.

This was particularly evident with respect to two countries: the USA and Germany. Whilst the Russians made considerable efforts to interest the Germans in an expansion of trade, they cut their purchases in the United States from October 1930 to March

1931 by 44.8 per cent compared with the same period in 1929-30.[41] There were several reasons behind this decision to shift orders from one country to the other. Firstly, there was a feeling that the Soviet Union had gone overboard in pursuit of US technology – *"the reconsideration of our amerikanomaniya"*, as *Ekonomicheskaya Zhizn'* expressed it.[42] Alone this would have been insufficient, were it not for two major political considerations which moved to the forefront of concern in 1930. Not only had increased trade with the USA failed to elicit diplomatic recognition, it had also undermined the strongest argument for recognition – access to the Russian market.[43] In addition, the grave deterioration in Soviet – German relations during the spring of 1930 presented an opportunity for France to exploit, and German equivocation over the Briand plan came as a clear reminder to Moscow that unless effective counter-measures were taken, Berlin might easily succumb to the blandishments of the French.

The Germans were now especially vulnerable economically, dazed by the Depression and further weakened by attempting to meet reparations payments under the Young Plan. Germany had traditionally been the Soviet Union's best trading partner and this was not merely due to their political intimacy. It was also attributable to the neat complementarity of the two economies – the Germans importing raw materials and exporting manufactures, the Russians the reverse. The effect of the Depression was to accentuate German dependence on the Russian market, whilst simultaneously reducing their purchases from the Soviet Union. With an economy running at only just over half capacity, its demand for raw materials dropped steeply, whilst the collapse of both domestic and international markets left German manufacturers with few clients. Germany was therefore prepared to offer better credit to Russian purchasers than any other country,[44] at a time when the imposition of trade sanctions by France further stimulated Russian interest in the German market.

Pre-empting Narkomindel and Narkomvneshtorg (Foreign Trade Commissariat) moves to open government-to-government negotiations, Ordzhonikidze, Politburo member and head of Vesenkha (the All-Union Council of National Economy), announced his intention to deal with German industrialists personally.[45] The leading figures from firms such as Krupps, AEG, Siemens and others, were invited to Moscow for talks, arriving on the 28 February 1931.[46] Ordzhonikidze was there to greet them and talks soon began. But whilst the leading economic potentate took a dominant role, political considerations loomed in the background. The Narkomindel's unofficial yet authoritative weekly, *Moskauer Rundschau*, gloated over the discomfort the visit caused in Paris and Washington. "One can say without doubt that instead of this trip the French press would have preferred Germany to interest itself in an economic blockade of the USSR, a blockade under the leadership of France and for French interests", wrote "Moskwitsch" on the 1 March, adding: "Equally indubitable is the fact that the American press would have preferred it if the trip had not taken place and the United States was able to take over a monopoly in the supply of the necessary machines, work-benches etc. to the USSR".[47] After only a temporary disturbance in negotiations, caused by excessive Soviet demands for credit, an agreement was eventually signed in Berlin on the 14 April.[48] As a result the Russians agreed to increase their demand for German goods by 300 million Marks, during the period from April to the end of August, aided by credits extended for up to an unprecedented 28 months.[49] Reflecting on the significance of the agreement, *Izvestiya* described it as a demonstration of "realism in politics".[50] The Russians certainly felt that they had gained the upper hand, for when, three months later, the German Centre Party's mouthpiece, *Germania*, floated the idea that Germany might join in an economic boycott of the USSR, *Izvestiya* took some pleasure in reminding its editor of the dilemma he faced:

what remains for him is either to support the German Communists – through increasing unemployment, or the USSR – through providing credits for exports.[51]

*   *   *

Foreign Communist Parties lay at the end of another arm of the Soviet state, and the Comintern, whilst retaining its own *raison d'être*, was also frequently wheeled in to protect and advance Russian interests. "Alongside the policy of peace carried out by the USSR ... the special determination of the international proletariat to fight against imperialist war and in defence of the

USSR is a most important factor preventing war", *Kommuni-sticheskii Internatsional* resolutely declared.[52] Yet, contrary to what one might have expected, work of this kind long remained a haphazard and relatively uncoordinated activity. Little was done by most Communist Parties other than mouth the appropriate slogans in demonstrations on the 1 August – an International Day Against Imperialist War. Exhortations from the Comintern executive committee during the war scare in the spring of 1930 "to expose energetically, now more than ever before, the interventionist plans of the imperialists and organise and head the movement of the proletariat *against* war"[53] left Communists abroad unmoved. A special July 1930 edition of the Comintern journal attempted to rectify this grave deficiency.[54] The shining example presented to all sections was that of the French Communist Party (PCF), which in 1929 instituted a system for gathering information about the country's war plans and military potential. It consisted of a network of "worker correspondents", who would write to *l'Humanité* from the factory or military unit, with information which the Party secretariat could then pass on to Moscow. In any language this amounted to espionage. As such it laid the PCF open to prosecution for treason, and led to the imprisonment of most of the party's leadership between 1929 and 1930, quite apart from its deleterious effects on patriotic voters. What the Comintern now advocated in July 1930 was an extension of this perilous practice to other countries:

> Workers in ordnance factories, the metallurgical and chemical industries must observe the course of production in their enterprises with the greatest attention for any change or innovation. They must watch that their enterprises are not used for *undercover military production*, that components for weapons and other military items are not being manufactured under the guise of some inoffensive label.

Similarly those working on or near transportation systems were instructed to exercise vigilance, as were those living in frontier regions. This was also essential in the "neutral" countries, whose *"industry and railroads"* could prove as important as "the armies themselves".[55] It was up to each Communist to expose "imperialist military preparations in *his own* country, in *his own* sector of industry or in *his own* part of the country".[56]

Given the dangers that hailed from France, the Russians naturally expected most from the PCF. But they were to be disappointed. During the agitation over the Kutepov affair, *l'Humanité* had rapidly expressed the party's solidarity with Moscow, stressing the Soviet Union's unique importance as "the socialist fatherland of all the oppressed".[57] When the head of Royal Dutch-Shell, Deterding – a longstanding bogey to the Russians – arrived by special plane from London at the end of March 1930, it provoked a hysterical outburst, as "workers and peasants" were called on to "Rise in Defence of the Soviet Union".[58] The introduction of restrictions on trade with Russia then prompted warnings of "armed aggression"[59] and was described as "a Direct Blow Against the Workers".[60] But, decapitated by the incarceration of its leadership for most of the year and demoralised by police harassment, the PCF's only contribution to the defence of the Soviet Union appears to have been verbal. It was therefore severely castigated at the XI plenum of the Comintern's executive committee (26 March–11 April 1931) for lack of effort.[61] Although regarded as a necessary adjunct to Litvinov's diplomatic manoeuvres, the anti-war movement in France and elsewhere was still very much in its infancy.

The French obsession inevitably also underlined the importance of maintaining the Rapallo relationship with Germany — a cornerstone in the structure of Soviet security. The visit of top German industrialists and the signature of a new agreement on trade and payments had come as welcome news. But the overall direction of Berlin's foreign policy still gave Moscow cause for alarm; much now depended on developments in Germany's domestic political situation.

6 The Place of Germany in Soviet Policy: 1930–31

From the onset of the Depression until 1933, German politics increasingly became polarised between two extremes: Communism and Fascism. Both tendencies were a product of the slump and the iniquities of the Versailles peace settlement. Existing German Governments, whether headed by Social Democrat or Centre Party politicians, sought a solution in closer integration with the victor Powers, aided by British and US mediation. The consequences for Moscow were viewed with great alarm by the Soviet leadership, supremely anxious to maintain the divide between those who had won and those who had lost in World War I as a proven guarantee against the formation of an anti-Soviet coalition. Soviet hopes therefore naturally turned on the polarisation of German domestic politics. But the prospects for a Communist-led coup in Berlin were too uncertain to be gambled upon, and although others, particularly at Comintern headquarters, may not have shared his outlook, Litvinov ably voiced sentiments which were undoubtedly shared by Stalin when he told the British ambassador that: "The Soviets wanted no revolution in Germany or elsewhere today; world revolution was undoubtedly 'on their books' but for the moment they were entirely concentrated on the five-year plan and wished to show concrete results in their own country as the best form of propaganda". These views were, he added, "shared by 'higher quarters'" – clearly a reference to Stalin and his colleagues.[1]

This did not imply that the German Communist Party (KPD) was of no use to Soviet interests, though Litvinov personally may well have had his doubts. But it did mean that its value could be compared with that of its natural enemy – the extreme Right – given that the focus of Moscow's concerns was anti-Western and above all anti-French, rather than directed towards social revolution within Germany. It was also by no means unprecedented for Soviet leaders to turn to the extreme Right in Germany as a safeguard against the country's desertion to the West. It was this that lay behind Soviet military collaboration with the Reichswehr, and during a previous period of great uncertainty – the Ruhr crisis of 1923 – with the threat of French hegemony menacing Europe should military intervention against Germany succeed, the Russians had instructed the KPD to co-operate in a common front with the fledgling National Socialist Party (NSDAP). This required some justification in terms other than crude realpolitik. Firstly came the revelation that "Fascism represents, not a clique of officers, but a broad, though contradictory, popular movement";[2] and secondly consolation was sought in the unjustified belief that its very amorphousness was a sign of weakness rather than strength. Although the Russians continued to urge on the KPD in its rivalry for power with the NSDAP, their overriding mistrust of the German Government and its Social Democrat supporters ensured that the Nazis and the Communists were seen as complements rather than polar opposites where Soviet state interests were concerned. For whilst the Nazis promised anti-Communist policies at home, they did at least also promise anti-Western policies abroad.

The Nazis first met with success at the local elections on the 17 November 1929, and on the 14 January 1930 National Socialist Wilhelm Frick became Minister of the Interior in the Thuringian Government. But few were inclined to take the Nazis seriously. Even the Italians were of the opinion that their leader Hitler "can not be considered a capable and serious politician" and that the party itself was trapped in a blind alley;[3] the British, too, emphasised that the significance of Nazi electoral successes "under the leadership of the half-mad and ridiculously dangerous demagogue Hitler" should "not be exaggerated".[4] It is scarcely surprising, therefore, that the German Communists themselves should strike a similar note. "It seems to us", wrote one KPD commentator, "that nationalist Fascist demagogy, bankrupted in the face of the unemployed movement, has already passed its most dangerous phase for us".[5] Furthermore in Moscow a similar assertion was reinforced by something far more insidious. An editor of *Kommunisticheskii Internatsional*, Martynov, went so far as to argue that the Nazis were to be regarded as a positive feature in that they helped to smash Social Democracy, clearing the road for the KPD. For him Fascism represented the death pangs of capitalism. Fascisisation was "incapable of stopping the revolutionary process". It merely bred "sharper forms of struggle by the revolutionary proletariat" and this was "a necessary precondition for its decisive victory".[6]

Thus those most concerned to further the German revolution – militants in the Comintern – were lulled into false complacency about National Socialism, whilst their superiors in the Soviet leadership, to the extent that they were aware of the issues, were at the very least ambiguous in their attitudes towards the Nazis. Even when a Nazi victory at the Saxon Landtag elections in June 1930[7] belied the extravagant optimism of KPD commentators, it led to no serious reappraisal of attitudes. On the contrary, Molotov's report on the Comintern to the XVI Party Congress that summer touched on the Nazi victory, but failed to draw any lessons from it,[8] whilst Stalin ignored the subject altogether.[9] Relations with the German Government had by then eased somewhat from their crisis point in the spring,[10] but the Russians still felt extremely uneasy about Berlin's continuing loyalty to the Rapallo relationship. The NSDAP's nationalist and anti-French agitation was therefore not unwelcome. Moscow also considered that the amorphous nature of the movement – particularly the continuous collisions between the nationalistic and the more socialist-inclined tendencies – was a weakness the KPD could successfully exploit. *Pravda* was especially concerned that the Communists should win over the nationalists:

The national Fascists have made political capital for themselves by having from the first begun (and are still carrying on) a bombastic, totally hypocritical, *nationalistic* campaign 'against the Young Plan' ... The basic task which now faces *the Communist Party of Germany in the struggle with national Fascism*, consists in *tearing the mask off the national Fascists as fighters for the national independence of the German people*, in order to counterpoise to their empty and lying demagogy a real revolutionary programme for the liberation of the toiling masses of Germany from the yoke of Young Plan pillage.[11]

The Reichstag was dissolved on the 18 July 1930, after the SPD withdrew its support for the Brüning Government, a Centre Party coalition which had replaced its Social Democrat predecessor at the end of March. National elections were called for the 14 September. There the Nazis achieved phenomenal results. The SPD lost seats, though it retained 143 – sufficient to support another coalition. The Communists now held 77 seats, an increase of 23. But the Nazis soared from a mere 12 to 107 seats. They also rose in Moscow's estimation, for although the NSDAP represented "the bourgeoisie", it had successfully used *"anti-capitalist slogans"*, convincing voters, "especially the young", that the Nazis were "fighters for the social liberation of the masses, for the overthrow of the Versailles treaty and the Young Plan yoke".[12] Then on the 21 September the Italian Fascist newspaper *Tribuna* published an interview given in Berlin by Graf Reventlow, head of the NSDAP in Northern Germany. He stated that a Franco-German rapprochement would damage the country's interests, by subjugating it to French domination. "Germany", he argued, "must orient itself not towards the West, but towards the East and South. Towards the East means towards Russia because we, in our economic and foreign policy, consider it necessary to take into account Russia's might".[13]

The September 1930 elections therefore had something positive to offer the Russians. Its *"results . . . promise great difficulties for French imperialism . . . the appearance in the European arena of a powerful imperialist competitor in the form of German neo-imperialism does not fit into its plans"*, *Pravda* emphasised.[14] The resurgence of German nationalism not only gave Moscow the promise of a more reliable ally now that France was imposing economic sanctions – announced early that October – it also became vital insurance against a Franco-German rapprochement. In retrospect it is clear that Soviet fears on this score were exaggerated – too many obstacles still lay strewn across its path – but they none the less contained an element of truth. This became apparent after the formation of a new government in France under the premiership of Pierre Laval, whom the Russians otherwise despised as "an inveterate place-seeker".[15] On the 23 February Berthelot, general secretary at the Quai d'Orsay, called in von Hoesch, the German ambassador, to air the idea of a comprehensive settlement between the two countries.[16] The Russians sensed that something was in the wind when on the 7 February an article appeared in *l'Europe Nouvelle* containing the suggestion that German reparations payments to France be cut in return for US concessions on French debts and the conclusion of a

"Franco-German military agreement" which would form the basis of a lasting peace between the two countries.[17]

The Russians had no choice but to wait upon events in Germany for resurgent nationalism to affect foreign policy. At the same time, however, the Narkomindel had to make the most of the existing situation. The first task was to seek a commitment from the German Government to renew the Berlin treaty (Rapallo's successor), and secondly, to bring about detente with Paris. The Berlin treaty was the only written guarantee the Russians had that committed Germany to non-participation in hostile combinations.[18] But by raising this issue and eliciting a far from enthusiastic response from the other side, Litvinov and his masters were left as insecure as before. The Germans agreed on renewal but demanded the right to abrogate the treaty at only six, or at most twelve, months' notice;[19] in contrast the Soviets stipulated a five-year moratorium on abrogation.[20] Still uncertain of the Germans, the Russians now proffered an olive branch to the French. At the sixth Congress of Soviets on the 8 March Molotov declared that "we are prepared to continue our efforts towards strengthening our mutual relations if we see a genuine readiness on the part of the French for an improvement in Franco-Soviet relations".[21] This was then followed up by Litvinov two days later in conversation with Herbette, prior to the latter's final departure for France. Here Litvinov went one step further than the wary Molotov: "France's military alliances still remain an obstacle of a sort", he pointed out, "but beyond this obstacle I do not see any objective reasons at all which would hinder the establishment of genuinely normal and even more intimate relations between ourselves and France".[22] The trouble was, of course, that the French Government would have to become obsessively anxious about German revanchism to accept such an offer. That time had not yet come, and the trial of the 'Industrial Party' still left a bad taste in their mouths; so they were loath to respond.[23]Indeed, the Quai d'Orsay's initial reaction was entirely negative:

> Faced with the Soviet menace, France has reacted instinctively in the necessary way to defend its well-being (*équilibre*) and its traditions. In issuing the decree of the 3 October it has, on the one hand, affirmed France's will when confronted with the will of the Soviet Union and it has attempted to protect French

agriculture. And was it not Lenin who declared that the small peasant proprietor was the greatest enemy of Bolshevism? In making a move in favour of agriculture, the French Government has shown that it intended to strengthen the centre of resistance of France against Bolshevism.

The conclusion drawn was that France should conclude no agreements with the USSR, whether economic or political, since this would deprive it of "freedom when in the near future the USSR will become a much more serious preoccupation than today for the 'capitalist Powers'". The opinion was also expressed that France should take diplomatic action "with the aim of preparing a plan for the future which will crystallise on the day the Soviet menace becomes clearer and more substantial". However, these words were not as ominous as they seemed. The only concrete step recommended was a move to dissuade Germany from providing the Russians with trade credits.[24]

It took the announcement of the Austro-German customs union on the 21 March to stir France from its intransigence. At first Moscow gave the union only a cautious welcome[25] – after all, the Russians had little interest in bolstering the power of a German Government so unenthusiastic about the future of the Rapallo relationship. But as French outcry at the news became increasingly strident, *Pravda* was moved to reflect with some relief that "the Austro-German agreement has with new and ... unprecedented acuteness *exposed the contradictions between the victors and the vanquished and revealed a significant weakening of the Versailles system*".[26] A bold act of defiance, simultaneously infringing the stipulations of the Versailles settlement and undermining the Briand plan, the customs union proved a grave embarrassment to France's Foreign Minister and threatened his prospects at the forthcoming Presidential elections. The Russians were now needed as a counter-balance. On the 20 April Berthelot asked to see Dovgalevsky. The latter was, however, too ill to visit the Quai and, much to the polpred's surprise, Berthelot hurried around to the Soviet embassy. Here he proposed simultaneous but unconnected negotiations for a non-aggression pact and commercial agreement.[27] This suggestion made Dovgalevsky more than a little suspicious since the experience of other countries in trade negotiations with France was that such talks would "drag on for many months, if not years". These doubts

were confirmed by Berthelot's reference to the "attacks to which
Briand was subjected recently in connexion with the Austro-
German protocol for a customs union". He spoke in the same
breath about "the desirability of concluding Briand's career at
the Ministry of Foreign Affairs with a brilliant coup (*acte d'éclat*)
such as the liquidation of the Franco-Soviet conflict". In his
subsequent despatch to Moscow Dovgalevsky voiced his deep
suspicions. Drawing Krestinsky's attention to the imminence of
the French Presidential elections, the failure of the Franco-Italian
naval negotiations, and the announcement of the customs union,
Dovgalevsky wondered whether Briand genuinely sought a pact
and trade agreement "or whether it was merely important for him
to make this move, obtain our consent, and then delay the opening
of the talks or even open them in the first half of May so as to
sabotage them later under plausible pretexts".[28] Although wide of
the mark in many respects, there was some justification for this
interpretation. The Ministry of Commerce actually desired some
sort of accomodation with the USSR, whereas the Quai could
scarcely conceal its distaste at the whole idea.[29] French behaviour
then merely reinforced existing Soviet suspicions. When talks of
an exploratory nature opened, Berthelot immediately attempted
to alter the understanding upon which they were based. This
drove Dovgalevsky – usually noticeably more Francophile than his
colleagues in Moscow – to the bitter reflection that "even having
stenographers present is insufficient when talking with my
partners".[30] Soviet bewilderment was equally apparent when
Litvinov encountered Briand at the European commission in
Geneva on the 22 May. He found the French Foreign Minister full
of bonhomie, but totally uninformed about the negotiations in
Paris.[31]

Mistrust of the French was only partly compensated for by the
signature of a protocol extending the life of the Berlin treaty on
the 24 June 1931 – the end-result of negotiations being a
compromise specifying a two-year moratorium on denunciation
and one year's notice.[32] The fact that the protocol was not ratified
until Hitler came to power testified to the continuing frailty of the
Rapallo relationship. This was apparent even at the time of
signature. A wave of bankruptcies was hitting the financial
markets of Europe. It began with the closing of the Austrian
Credit-Anstalt early in May and by mid-June the outflow of
foreign exchange had precipitated a major financial crisis in

Germany. Anxious about the future social and political consequences of financial collapse — the danger of revolution was
referred to by Under-Secretary of State William Castle on the 13
June[33] — the USA finally stepped in with proposals for a
moratorium on reparations payments, made public by President
Hoover a week later.[34] The French were none too pleased at this,
but succumbed to US pressure on the 6 July. And whilst the
Russians were as nervous of revolution in Germany as everyone
else, they liked the idea of American intervention even less. In
this respect two comments are worth quoting. The first comes
from *l'Humanité*, which appeared on the 8 July with an editorial
bitterly entitled: "The Young Plan In Crisis – The gendarme of
Europe and the imperialism of the electric chair have come to an
agreement". The second appears in *Izvestiya*, above the signature
of Radek, once again a prominent commentator on foreign
affairs, who now warned that: *"were the United States to succeed
in obtaining a reduction in the contradictions between the
imperialist Powers of Europe, then this would facilitate the
creation of a united front directed against the USSR"*.[35]

Such fears were confirmed with the arrival in France on the 18
July of the first German Chancellor to visit Paris since the war.
Although the Russians could congratulate themselves that, so far
at least, with prominent banks still closing their doors, the
"Hoover 'miracle'" had "not saved the German economy",[36] they
were also only too conscious of the fact that Germany's financial
collapse was tilting the scales to the advantage of the French. The
power of France alone stood untouched by the surrounding
chaos. It was inevitable that its privileged position should be used
to wring political concessions from Germany. "Never have we had
a stronger position", wrote Berthelot that summer.[37] In return for
a ten-year loan, the French sought Germany's acceptance of all
the postwar frontiers or, at the very least, a German commitment
to abstain from rearmament; they also offered a pact of non-
aggression and consultation.

The Russians were apparently well aware that this or
something similar was on the agenda. An editorial in *Pravda*
coinciding with Brüning's arrival in Paris warned that: "The
German bourgeoisie might capitulate. However, the German
proletariat, the German working masses cannot and will not
capitulate, cannot and will not put up with the reinforcement of
the Versailles chains, the subordination of Germany to French

imperialism, the inclusion of Germany in an anti-Soviet front."[38]
In the event nothing came of the French proposals. But Paris did
not entirely give up hope. Moscow had good reason to worry.

*   *   *

A vivid indicator of Moscow's state of mind was the effusive and
otherwise inexplicable comment lavished on the signature of a
non-aggression pact with Afghanistan. Ibrahim Beg had crossed
the Oxus in March 1931, joined with the Basmachis at Dushambe
and cut up two battalions of Soviet troops. Moscow then sent in
reinforcements and, fearing reprisals across the frontier, the
Afghan Premier approached the British Minister in Kabul with a
request for consultations in the event of Soviet aggression.[39] As
much as the British relished rebellion in Soviet Central Asia, they
did not take kindly to the idea of the fighting spilling over into
Afghanistan, thereby disturbing the peace of Southern Asia, with
untold consequences for British dominion in India. London
therefore decided that the time had come to have Beg arrested so
as to "remove any excuse for the violation of Afghan territory".[40]
But the Russians succeeded in capturing him before this was
possible, thus paving the way for the signature of a non-
aggression pact on the 24 June. The pact itself testifies to Russian
concerns early that summer. It was almost identical to the
previous agreement of August 1926, except in respect of article
four, which now ran as follows:

> Each of the high contracting parties states that it has had and
> has no secret or open obligations in relation to one or several
> states which would contradict the existing treaty, and that in
> the course of the whole period of activity of this treaty it will
> not enter into such treaties and agreements, which would
> contradict the existing treaty.[41]

To the Russians a month later its significance lay far beyond the
parochial politics of Central and Southern Asia, as *Moskauer
Rundschau* pointed out on the 19 July (the day after Brüning's
arrival in Paris):

> At a time when the world economic crisis is growing ever more

severe, the danger of war becoming ever more real, with
lingering plans for the economic isolation of the USSR and the
preparation of an intervention against the Soviet Union, the
pact with Kabul confirms the unshakable determination of the
Soviet Union to maintain peace and to continue its economic
construction unhindered.[42]

*   *   *

The Russians held out little hope that the French Government
would follow the Afghan example while there was still the
possibility that Germany could be brought to its knees. When the
Franco-German talks then shifted to Britain on the 20 July to
draw in the Americans and the British, *Pravda* nervously wrote
of "The London Conspiracy".[43] In these circumstances the
Russians continued to count on German nationalism, whether
exploited by the KPD or the extreme Right, as a means of
exerting pressure on Brüning. Reliance on the Right was further
justified when Hitler and the German Nationalist Party jointly
sent a telegram to the German delegation in London on the 21
July. It warned that "the entire national opposition *will consider
itself in no way bound* by concessions made by Brüning in relation
to France".[44] This was the setting in which the Soviet leadership
was called upon to arbitrate between two factions within the KPD
Politburo. On the one side stood Neumann, the enfant terrible of
the German Communist movement, who favoured joining the
NSDAP in their demand for a plebiscite to oust the Social
Democrats (SPD) from the government of Prussia. On the other
side lay the more cautious elements, who recognised that the
threat from the Nazis was at least equal to that from the SPD.[45]
Neumann had been arguing since the spring that, with the Nazis
in decline, little was to be feared from that quarter.[46] This
argument, combined with the evident utility of nationalist
agitation from the extreme Right, evidently proved difficult to
oppose in Moscow. There, opinion within both the Comintern
and the Narkomindel was divided. Manuilsky, heading the Soviet
delegation to the Comintern, apparently opposed co-operation
with the Fascists. Yet the dominant view, promulgated by Knorin
who headed the Central European secretariat, matched that of
Neumann.[47] At the Narkomindel a "pessimistic" Litvinov feared

"the possibility of some form of Fascist government emerging in Germany", whereas his immediate subordinate Krestinsky was not nearly so worried.[48] Evidently the French obsession was too strong for Stalin and his colleagues to resist. In their eyes the SPD was nothing more than a fifth column for the French. The decision therefore went in Neumann's favour. On the 22 July TASS reported an ultimatum which the KPD put to the Social Democrat administration of Prussia in the sure knowledge that it would be rejected, and so it was.[49] On the 9 August the plebiscite took place, and, although hailed by the Communists as a success, it failed in its aim. The Social Democrats remained in place.[50] Evidently under Litvinov's influence, *Moskauer Rundschau* was more honest than the remainder after Soviet press, arguing that: "From a foreign policy standpoint the 9 August was evidence that the German bourgeoisie is ready to knuckle under to foreign creditors – with French imperialism in the front rank".[51]

It was at this stage, and after the mutual abrogation of existing trade restrictions on the 11 July, that the French Government, evidently despairing of success with respect to Germany, took the hesitant step of initialling a non-aggression pact with the USSR on the 10 August.[52] But the furore this provoked in the French press of almost every political persuasion evidently took the Government by surprise. France now drew back, politely but firmly explaining to the Russians that no further progress could be expected until a similar pact had been agreed with Poland.[53]

The Poles had originally expressed an interest in signing a non-aggression pact in the late autumn of 1930, under the impact of NSDAP election successes. On the 19 November the Polish ambassador in Ankara had approached Surits, his Soviet counterpart, with proposals for the normalisation of relations, the establishment of diplomatic relations between Moscow and Bucharest, the non-renewal of the Polish-Romanian alliance, and the conclusion of a non-aggression pact even in the event of unsuccessful negotiations between the Russians and the Romanians.[54] This abrupt volte-face proved extremely short-lived, however. The Soviets grasped the bait, and Antonov-Ovseenko, polpred in Warsaw, went along to see Count Raczynski, head of the Eastern department at the Polish Foreign Ministry, to propose the resumption of conversations on this subject. But Raczynski, evidently in response to a shift in opinion at higher levels, appeared reluctant to do anything prior to the renewal of the Polish-Romanian treaty of alliance. Thus any question of negotiations with the Russians had to be postponed until at least the end of the year.[55] Although the Russians were none too pleased at this,[56] these were the first indications that, under the impact of growing revanchism in Germany, Poland might reconsider its place in the French alliance system and along with it the hitherto unwavering hostility that characterised its attitude towards the USSR. For the moment, however, concern to maintain the alignment with Bucharest hindered any further progress in this direction, and the realisation that Nazi election successes were having no appreciable impact on German foreign policy evidently deprived Warsaw of any sense of urgency in regulating relations with Moscow. Indeed in March 1931 Berlin had ratified the commercial treaty concluded with Warsaw early in 1930. It was not until France moved to initial its pact with the USSR that the Poles felt compelled to act. On the 23 August, possibly after further soundings by Antonov-Ovseenko, they presented the Russians with a draft agreement on non-aggression.[57]

The French explained their delay in signing the non-aggression pact with Russia as an unfortunate imposition forced upon them by the Poles. But, as Berthelot made clear later, Poland had made no objection to the idea that France continue with signature. It was, in fact, the French themselves who originated this linkage,[58] and this appears to have stemmed from the reluctance of the conseil d'état under Laval to pursue matters any further – at least in the near future. A memorandum written after the event by the Quai's Direction des affaires politiques et commerciales contains the following passage:

> Before submitting the projected non-aggression pact to the Minister of Foreign Affairs and reaching a final decision on the text, the Government wanted to take a further precaution in making it conditional upon the opinion of the Polish, Romanian, Finnish, Latvian and Estonian Governments, and on their signature.[59]

This was only partly true. The other side to the story is that, as Berthelot informed the Greek ambassador to Paris on the 18 August, France was still looking for a rapprochement with Germany at Soviet expense.[60] Evidently arguing against some who held to a different opinion, a writer in *Kommunisticheskii Internatsional* insisted that "it would be the grossest error to deny the possibility of military co-operation between Germany and France against the USSR by counting on ... contradictions existing between the two countries".[61] The continuation of such fears meant that Moscow's backhanded indulgence towards the NSDAP in Germany would persist. As *Pravda* noted on the 11 October: "France fears that with the arrival of the Fascists in power their social demagogy will bring about a growth in the anti-Versailles sentiments of the petty bourgeois masses."[62]

Despite these continuing anxieties, by the autumn the tension that had characterised the Soviet position abroad had eased considerably. The renewal of the Berlin treaty and the initialling of a non-aggression pact with France showed there were cracks in the armour of capitalism; a welcome indication that the exploitation of differences amongst the imperialist Powers was at last bearing fruit. The Russians had successfully warded off the threat of an international economic blockade and, with the Depression settling in, they had every hope of continuing to take advantage of their demand for goods that could find no buyer in the markets of the West. A telling symptom of the relative improvement in the USSR's international position was, as Litvinov noted when attending the League European Commission early in September, "a considerable reduction in outward hostility towards us. Even the Genevan press has this time abstained from any attacks".[63] But before the month was out, a new threat had materialised on the horizon, which added further unexpected complications for Soviet foreign policy.

7 The Manchurian Crisis: 1931

On the 18 September 1931 Japanese forces launched an unauthorised assault on North-Eastern China (Manchuria). The effects of the Depression in Japan and the resurgence of nationalism in China had combined to break the rotting tether which bound the army on the Kwantung peninsula to the restraining hand of Shidehara diplomacy.[1] Moscow was directly interested in the crisis because the pretext for aggression was the explosion of a bomb at Mukden on the South Manchurian Railway. Further up the line lay the Chinese Eastern Railway (CER), which the Soviet Government had inherited from its predecessors and defended from forcible seizure by the Nationalists (Kuomintang) and their allies in 1929. Sustained possession of the railway testified to continued preoccupations about the balance of power in the region,[2] originally aroused by Japanese military intervention in the Soviet Far East from 1918 to 1922, bolstered by Britain's bombardment of Nanking in 1927 and consolidated by the consequent conversion of the Kuomintang into a partner of the West. The Russians were not merely passive observers, however. They actively sought the unification of an anti-imperialist China and this, despite the debilitated condition of the Chinese Communist Party (CCP), played its part in turning Tokyo against Moscow, at a time when the Depression accentuated Japanese dependence on Manchuria as a secure and vital source of raw materials, as a focus for trade and investment, as well as a place of settlement for "excess" population; likewise the sight of Eastern Siberia's vast expanse also whetted the appetites of the land hungry in huddled Japan.

For the Russians, the Japanese occupation of Manchuria took place against a background of protracted difficulties in the Soviet Far East. Soviet agriculture generally was in crisis, and the harvest of 1931 was poor. As Alec Nove has observed: "The peasants were demoralized. Collective farms were inefficient, the horses slaughtered or starving, tractors as yet too few and poorly maintained, transport facilities inadequate, the retail distribution system (especially in rural areas) utterly disorganized by an over-precipitate abolition of private trade".[3] Famine was on its way. The disruption caused by collectivisation, which had been renewed with vigour in the winter of 1930/1, engendered unrest in the Soviet Far East, as in Russia proper, except that it appears to have become more intractable there than elsewhere. Commanding the Special Far Eastern Army, set up on the 6 August 1929 to meet the threat to the CER from the Kuomintang, was General Blyukher. His overriding aim was to develop the region into a self-sufficient economic unit which could support its own defence.[4] It was evidently this that brought him into conflict with Moscow and led, by late November 1930, to talk of his arrest on charges of conspiring against the Party leadership.[5] Denied by the Soviet Government, the rumours proved difficult to dispel,[6] and re-emerged in May and June of 1931.[7] Arrested or no, the General had clearly fallen from favour, but only temporarily, for he had become a figure with an international reputation as well as considerable domestic popularity as a result of his defence of the CER in 1929. The Politburo evidently decided to take his grievances seriously. On the 11 March 1931 Sovnarkom granted privileges to military personnel discharged from the Far Eastern Army settling in the region.[8] More was to follow.

In late July Voroshilov began an extensive tour of garrisons, factories and collective farms in Siberia and the Soviet Far East, a tour which lasted nearly two months, including what appears to have been a public reconciliation with Blyukher, when he awarded the General the Order of Lenin and the Order of the Red Star on the 6 August.[9] Although most of the Soviet press had little concrete to say of Voroshilov's visit, *Izvestiya*'s comment nearly a week later is worthy of quotation, for behind the customary clichés lurked the unanswered question: why did the Far East merit so much of the Commissar's time and attention?

> Voroshilov's trip to the Far East has activated to an even greater extent the creative efforts of the worker and collective farm masses on the battle-front of socialist construction. In addition, Voroshilov's visit to garrisons and military units has

no less significance for a subsequent increase in the military capability of troops from the Special Far Eastern Army and its transformation into a truly invincible force, firmly stationed on the frontier of the Soviet Far East.

Voroshilov was also reported as having "made use of every day to become personally acquainted with the state of the troops, their living conditions and military preparedness".[10]

Circumstantial evidence indicates that the tour was prompted not merely by the demoralisation and discontent rife in the army and at its economic base, but also because the Russians could not rule out the possibility of an attack by Japan in the near future. Soviet Intelligence had intercepted a telegram from Lt.Col. Kasahara, the Japanese military attaché in Moscow, sent to the General Staff in March 1931. According to Kasahara's subsequent testimony sixteen years later, the proposals were "*ridiculed*" in Tokyo as "the opinions of an immature observer".[11] But the Russians were doubtless not privy to their reception in Japan. All they could be sure of was that in reviewing the USSR's military preparedness, Kasahara had concluded that "her war-operational capacity . . . in the broadest sense of the word, i.e., her economic power, her munitions industries, and her national unity, cannot yet be considered adequate". Referring to Japan, he added:

it will be her unavoidable destiny to clash with the USSR sooner or later. However, as mentioned above, considering the capacity of the USSR for national defence and the situation of the other Powers, the sooner the Soviet–Japanese war comes, the better for us. We must realize that with every day the situation develops more favorably for the USSR.

In short, I hope the authorities will make up their minds for a speedy war with the Soviet Union, and initiate policies accordingly. Taking into consideration the fact that the disadvantage of opening a war at present lies not on our side but on their side irrespective of which is better, peace or war, Japan, I believe, must adopt a strong policy against the USSR, firmly resolved not to flinch from war, and must here and now demand a radical solution to the fisheries problem and all the other questions.[12]

In these circumstances the Russians inevitably harboured suspicions that the Mukden incident might be the prelude to a more generalised conflict in the Far East. As soon as the news reached Moscow via TASS, Deputy Commissar for Foreign Affairs Karakhan called in the Japanese ambassador for an explanation, and emphasised that the Soviet Government attributed "the most serious significance" to these events. But Hirota was unforthcoming and told Karakhan nothing more than he already knew.[13] Japanese reticence also characterised Litvinov's unfruitful conversation with him three days later, much to the Commissar's annoyance.[14] This lack of information, disturbing though it undoubtedly was, did have its uses, however. For when Mo Teh-hui, the head of the Chinese Nationalist delegation in Moscow, called on Karakhan, he was informed that without more data the Soviet Government was unable to form a "final opinion" on events. The most the Deputy Commissar could offer were his sympathies and an assurance that Moscow would not further complicate China's position.[15] Relations between the Russians and the Chinese were still uncertain – hence Mo's presence in Moscow heading a delegation to resolve the CER dispute of 1929, which had resulted in the Soviet breach of relations with Nanking;[16] so the Russians had little incentive to become embroiled in a conflict with Japan on behalf of the Kuomintang. Lack of information was also a convenient excuse for the absence of press comment, though, once again, the real reason soon became apparent: a strong reluctance to confront Japan.

The first public expression of a Soviet viewpoint did not appear until the 25 September. *Pravda* generously apportioned criticism on all sides – to the Japanese, the League of Nations, the Americans and the Nanking Government – but whereas "sympathy" for the Chinese people was dutifully expressed, it was also made clear that the only force which could save them was "*the victory of the worker-peasant revolution in China under the leadership of the Chinese Communist Party*".[17] *Izvestiya*, on the other hand, saw something positive in the position of the United States. Secretary of State Stimson had informed Debuchi, the Japanese ambassador to Washington, that public confidence in the stability of Manchuria had already been shaken and that an indefinite occupation by Japanese troops would cause a further loss of confidence. Then, in a telegram to the League on the 24

September, he expressed his "wholehearted sympathy" with its attitude to the crisis and pointed out that he had "already urged the cessation of hostilities and a withdrawal from the present situation of danger".[18] "At a time when the League of Nations' position is one of de facto support for Japan, the USA's statement has to be considered an extremely direct warning addressed to Japan", *Izvestiya* argued hopefully.[19] Even when nothing concrete resulted from American protestations, the Russians continued to look expectantly in their direction for opposition to Japanese expansion. On the 18 October *Pravda* suggested that *"the Sino-Japanese conflict is changing into a US-Japanese one"*,[20] and as late as the end of November the Comintern's China specialist Pavel Mif wrote that "the USA lays claim to the whole of China and, more than any other country, does not want Japan strengthened. Therefore one cannot exclude the possibility that in the immediate future we will witness a severe exacerbation of contradictions, primarily between Japan and the USA".[21]

However, not only did the Americans prove reluctant to engage the Japanese without British support, and the collapse of sterling on the 21 September ensured that this would not be forthcoming (an event otherwise welcomed by the Russians),[22] but the Chinese Communists were not much help either. "The moment for the Japanese action was excellently chosen", as *Moskauer Rundschau* had pointed out,[23] and this applied equally to the situation within China as to the distractions of the Great Powers. The CCP was nominally still led from Shanghai, the industrial centre of China, but in reality it was almost exclusively concentrated in rural soviets much further south in Kiangsi province, hemmed in by the besieging forces of the Kuomintang. With what amounted to a civil war in progress, it was scarcely surprising that the CCP neglected the struggle against Japan taking place across the other side of the country. But Moscow, preoccupied with its own vulnerability vis-à-vis the Japanese, was intolerant of CCP negligence. Evidently in response to questions from the Kremlin, the Comintern secretariat cabled the CCP at the end of December 1931 asking for "a detailed report on the steps to develop a national struggle against imperialism". The programme that was required, the telegram continued, had to "aim at arming the people for a national revolutionary war to oppose Japanese imperialists and all other imperialists in order to win the liberation of the Chinese nation and to promote the independence and unification of China". In concrete terms, the Communists were instructed to "call on people throughout the country to defend China with armed force. Develop the strike movement. Through your pickets seize control over the movement for boycotting Japanese goods". Together with this went the instruction to further expand the Red Army and guerrilla warfare. Action on two fronts meant that they had to "stir up the peasant masses in Kuomintang-ruled areas" and also set up "mass anti-imperialist organizations". The revolutionary war "against the imperialists and the Kuomintang" was treated as one and the same war. Lastly, they had to "publicise proletarian international unity, especially with the revolutionary proletarians in Japan".[24]

But the response of the CCP was rather unhelpful. Its central committee published a resolution "concerning the Japanese imperialist occupation of Manchuria", describing the Manchurian incident as a sign that the dismemberment and colonisation of China by the imperialist Powers was now beginning. This would, the resolution argued, "have a decisive influence on future events in China". But the CCP appeared to regard this as a positive rather than a negative feature, arguing that it would "greatly facilitate the soviet movement and the Red Army and make ripe conditions for a nation-wide revolution". The incident had struck a new and significant blow at the rule of the Chinese bourgeoisie, which would "prompt the collapse and bankruptcy of Kuomintang rule, preparing the ground for opportune objective conditions for victorious revolutionary struggles".[25]

The Japanese Communist Party (JCP) responded more enthusiastically than its counterpart in China, though scarcely more effectively. Immediately after the Mukden incident it issued a declaration to "workers, peasants and soldiers" to "conclude an alliance with Chinese workers and peasants and rise up in struggle in the name of revolutionary solidarity", ending with this resounding call:

Demand that the army immediately leave Mukden and all places that have been occupied! Immediate withdrawal of the Japanese army and warships from China and Manchuria! Do not transport one soldier! Resist all the military moves of Japanese imperialism and Chinese reaction! Fight against the

new danger of an imperialist war! Co-operate with the Red
Army! Defend the USSR! Down with imperialist Japan! For a
soviet Japan![26]

But *Kommunisticheskii Internatsional* criticised the JCP's
successes in this field as "far from adequate",[27] though this was
hardly surprising in view of the harsh repression suffered at the
hands of the police since 1928, with the detention of 2000
members, followed in 1929 by another 295, in 1930–1500; and in
April 1931 alone there were 2000 "revolutionary workers and
peasants" arrested, in May – 1215, June – 1100, July – 803, and
August – 1500. All Communist organisations, including trade
unions and the League Against Imperialism, had been driven
underground.[28] Thus Comintern strictures about failure to take
advantage of "revolutionary perspectives" merely reeked of self-
deception, mitigated only by this uncharacteristic admission from
Comintern secretary Kuusinen:

> On the one hand, it has to be recognised that in the struggle
> against the war the Party has stood the test, acting as a true
> Bolshevik party. But, on the other hand, it is still a terribly
> weak party. Why hide this from ourselves? Why not recognise
> that a great part of our cadres are incarcerated, that a
> significant number of them have fallen victim to police
> provocations? This says how minimally prepared we were for
> this.[29]

The emasculation of the Japanese Communist Party and the
equivocal response of the Chinese Communists increasingly
worried Moscow as it became evident that a US-Japanese conflict
was less likely than a Soviet-Japanese one. Not only was there a
resurgence of Russian emigré activity under Ataman Semenov in
Manchuria aided by the Kwantung army command,[30] but the
Japanese were treating the Soviet Union quite differently from the
other Powers. Whereas communications between Tokyo and the
League, or even between Japan and the USA, were widely
publicised, the Japanese ignored the USSR, which left the
Russians "highly agitated". As Litvinov explained to Hirota, at
another meeting, on the 2 October, the Soviet Government was
"especially interested in the activity of White Guards and their
link with the Japanese command". Hirota was mistaken, Litvinov

warned, if he thought "that our public is less interested in the Manchurian events, than the League of Nations or American circles". The Russians might be "more circumspect, sharing the aim of their Government not to complicate the situation", but they could not remain "indifferent" to what was going on over the frontier in the Far East. The Soviet Government was not, he persisted, merely "interested" in the matter; it was also "worried" about it.[31]

The tactics the Russians now pursued were evidently the result of an awkward compromise between those pressing for a more active policy and those whose attention was focused on Europe, rating the Far East a lower priority (see below, p.81). For whilst trying to remove any grounds for conflict with Japan at one level, even at the cost of weakening Chinese resistance to their occupiers, Moscow also moved to bring all disagreements with Japan out into the open – even to the extent of publishing telegrams intercepted en route from the Japanese embassy to Tokyo. Japan accused the Russians of providing instructors to General Ma, then leading the resistance in Manchuria. Tokyo went so far as to warn the Soviet Union that if its forces were sent onto the CER, "this will worsen the atmosphere and aggravate the situation", obliging the Japanese to take "necessary defence measures". This ultimatum, along with the Soviet reply, were both released to the press by TASS at the end of October. The Soviet retort was framed in terms of innocent amazement at such accusations, coupled with the assertion that Moscow's policy was one of "strict non-interference", and adding that "a policy of military occupation, carried out in the form of so-called aid, is inconsistent with the pacific policy of the USSR and with the interests of universal peace".[32] But the Japanese continued to complain of Soviet aid to Ma. According to the Kwantung army command, not only were there Communist partisans appearing along the Soviet border, but from the 6 to the 8 November seventeen wagonloads of arms and ammunition came down the CER from a westerly direction, presumably the USSR. This prompted Moscow to instruct the management of the railway to prohibit arms shipments to either side in the conflict.[33] Evidently a reversal of policy, the Soviet consul in Harbin had difficulty in explaining this away to the Chinese representative, Chun Yu, on the 13 November 1931.[34] The Russian decision was based on the knowledge that the

Kwantung army were prepared to use any Soviet action as an excuse for restricting their control over the railway.[35]

The Soviet public had to wait a long time before a member of the Government delivered a speech dealing with the crisis in the Far East. The first occasion was on the 22 December, at a session of the central executive committee, when Molotov spoke on the international situation. It was immediately clear from the speech that the leadership's silence on the issue was no indication as to its lack of importance. On the contrary, it was the most crucial question of them all. The Soviet Union had to increase its vigilance, despite absorption "in the tasks of raising production". Moscow would continue to assert its basic principle that "we have no need of other land, but neither will we surrender a single inch of our land to anybody", whilst simultaneously answering all provocations with a policy of peace.[36] The careful counter-balancing of references to the need for vigilance with an emphasis on the danger of provocations showed once again that Moscow had no intention of being drawn into a conflict with Japan.[37]

An obvious extension of the Soviet Government's peace policy was to offer the Japanese a non-aggression pact. The occasion arose after the Japanese appointed Yoshizawa Foreign Minister, when he was en route back to Tokyo via Moscow. Guided by the knowledge that he had played a significant role in securing Japanese recognition of the USSR, signing the Peking treaty of 1925, the Russians naturally hoped that he could be persuaded to reverse the decline in relations between the two countries. Litvinov therefore pointed to all the non-aggression pacts concluded or currently being negotiated between the USSR and its neighbours, with the obvious exception of Japan. "We consider it necessary to remedy this omission", he told Yoshizawa, "otherwise a strange situation will result, whereby Japan will turn out to be the only neighbour with whom there exists no non-aggression pact". Such pacts were the expression of peace-loving policies. This was an especially opportune moment, when the future of Soviet–Japanese relations was the object of speculation in Europe and the United States. Signing such a pact would "end this speculation". Yoshizawa and Hirota were "taken by surprise" at this offer, but agreed to pass it on to Tokyo.[38] There, polpred Troyanovsky was also attempting to improve relations, this time by holding out the promise of economic concessions in return for an agreement to abstain from aggression against the USSR.[39]

However all Soviet offers went unanswered. The Japanese military continued as before to talk about the annexation of not only Soviet Sakhalin, but even the USSR's littoral and Kamchatka.[40] Meanwhile in Moscow Litvinov gloomily predicted to foreign diplomats that sooner or later Japan and the Soviet Union would be at war. This was not an immediate prospect, he stressed, but rather a general outlook on the future.[41] When questioned on their attitude towards the proposed pact, the Japanese evaded the point by insisting that all outstanding issues (such as fisheries) be settled first.[42] There were absolutely no signs that they were willing to put relations with Moscow on a better footing. On the contrary, in Manchuria the Kwantung army began to press the Russians for the right to use the CER in their operations against the Chinese.[43] The reply from Moscow was that this would not be possible without the permission of both the Soviet and Chinese Governments.[44] The Russians held to this position, despite Japanese pressure, up to the moment that the Chinese themselves eventually gave way to the demands of the Japanese.[45] However, before this point was reached, the Japanese began to seize control of stations along the railway. The first incident of this kind occurred at Shwangchengpu on the 4 February 1932.[46] When the Chinese finally agreed to Japan's demands, the Russians accompanied their own compliance with a warning that these demands infringed the Portsmouth treaty and a request that the Japanese respect the remaining articles of that agreement.[47] These included stipulations against the concentration of Japanese forces along the Russo-Korean frontier.[48]

Whilst making important concessions to the Japanese, the Russians also made efforts to ensure that the world knew just how badly Tokyo was behaving. On the 4 March *Izvestiya* published an editorial entitled "The Soviet Union and Japan", which included extracts from the Kasahara telegram, as well as from another telegram to the chief of staff giving an account of the views of Hirota expressed to Major-General Harada, then visiting Moscow. In this conversation Hirota is recorded as having said:

> Putting aside the question of whether or not Japan should make war against the Soviet Union, there is the need to take a strong policy [line] vis-à-vis the Soviet Union, with the resolve

to fight the USSR at any time necessary. The objective, however, should not be defense against Communism but, rather, the occupation of Far Eastern Siberia.[49]

Yet aside from issuing repeated protests to the Japanese, this was as far as Moscow felt able to go. The Russians had already embarked upon a seemingly endless series of concessions towards Japan, necessitated by economic and military weakness, a further sign of which was the attitude adopted towards the new puppet state of Manchukuo, set up by the Japanese in Manchuria. The Russians were asked to grant diplomatic recognition.[50] Moscow took its time before answering. Not until nine days after the message was received did Karakhan cable Slavutsky, the Soviet consul in Harbin, to give verbal acknowledgement of its receipt.[51] An interpreter from the consulate then informed the new regime of that fact.[52] Henceforth the Russians were to pursue a policy of de facto recognition, dictated by the concern to deprive the Japanese military of any opportunity to further infringe Soviet interests in the region.

This conciliatory line aroused strong opposition in Moscow. Apparently not only among the military, but also within the higher reaches of the Communist Party, there was concern at the consequent demoralisation of the Red Army and a strong desire to prevent the permanent presence of Japanese forces in Manchuria.[53] The prospect of continued appeasement was made easier to accept only on the assumption that by pursuing this course the Russians could swing opinion within Japan against the more militaristic and anti-Soviet elements. For the spring of 1932 was a time of heated debate not merely in Moscow. In Tokyo, too, controversy was difficult to conceal. Admiral Kato and Viscount Saito, the latter being chairman of the Japanese–Soviet Society, and Premier from May 1932, were working to reorient Japanese policy from its position of confrontation with Moscow.[54] As a result of the information he received from such sources, polpred Troyanovsky[55] concluded that the Japanese were unlikely to seek war with the USSR for the moment, at least, though "any significant change whatsoever in the international situation might easily bring about a war".[56]

Thus the crisis in the Far East made it ever more vital that the Soviets settle their relations with Europe and prevent the emergence of a coalition of Powers upon whom the Japanese could rely as future allies. At home it meant that the Russians had no choice but to focus their energies on increasing Soviet defence capabilities in the Far East, even at the expense of the five-year plan.

8 The Threat from Japan Takes Priority

Although Soviet appeasement of Japan stands in stark contrast to Moscow's foreign policy position prior to the Manchurian crisis, there was no lack of effort in the USSR's desperate search for a position of strength by both the mobilisation of military and economic resources at home and the mustering of other Communist Parties abroad to weaken Japan's capacity to wage war.

Thus Soviet forces in the Far East were substantially reinforced. By the end of 1931 the Politburo had decided on the creation of naval forces in the region; the 21 April 1932 therefore saw the birth of the Soviet fleet in the Pacific. On the 29 June the first submarine trials took place, but these new vessels did not enter service until late September.[1] On land the introduction of aircraft and tanks buttressed growing numbers of troops, estimates of which vary, but it appears that by the spring of 1932 there were at least 100 000 in total.[2] Moscow simultaneously attempted to make the region more self-sufficient economically. On the 16 March 1932 the Politburo ordered the creation of a special collective farm corps to:

> reinforce Soviet Far Eastern frontiers, bring the richest new virgin lands under the plough, guarantee supplies for the population of the Far East and the army, cut the exportation of grain and fats from Siberia to the Far East significantly and develop the economy of the Far East.[3]

However, autarchy was a distant goal. Mobilisation for defence was achieved only at great cost to the country as a whole, and at the expense of production targets in the five-year plan. As Stalin pointed out: "in view of the refusal of neighbouring countries to sign pacts of non-aggression with us, and of the complications that arose in the Far East, we were obliged, for the purpose of strengthening our defence, hastily to switch a number of factories to the production of modern defensive means".[4] According to British embassy sources, no less than sixty factories were, by March 1932, working for war production. Work at the Putilov munitions plant in Leningrad had been speeded up. The Mytishche factory, which normally repaired railway wagons, was now turned over to the production of gun limbers. In Rostov-on-Don, the factory producing agricultural machinery was partly switched to the construction of whippet tanks, whilst in Stalingrad the heavy artillery plant was working at high pressure.[5] At Geneva in the spring of 1932 Radek told British diplomats that the Soviet Union had spent "milliards" of roubles in the previous year on defence preparations. This had strained the country's resources and compelled the Russians to change their five-year plan. The whole output of the metallurgical industry, for example, had to be altered for defence production. Enough grain had had to be stored to supply the army for one year. All this, including the transportation required for moving supplies to the Far East, was said by Radek to account for the current "food shortage" and the "general tightening of conditions".[6] In fact famine had trodden its own lethal path to certain regions. The requisitioning of grain and meat involuntarily contributed to epidemics and starvation, and also to outbreaks of guerrilla fighting in areas like the Caucasus by May 1932;[7] by August the food supply in Leningrad had sunk to such parlous levels that a senior official of OGPU went so far as to admit to the British ambassador: "There's no bread, no meat, no fats – nothing."[8]

The threat posed by the Japanese advance gradually opened the way to a reorientation in the sectarian policies which had prevailed in the Comintern since 1928. However, with respect to the Chinese Communist Party (CCP), besieged by Kuomintang forces from November 1931, there was little scope for progress on this front. Considerable confusion therefore arose from the Comintern's attempts to encourage the unification of Chinese resistance to the Japanese invader. Even after a section of the Kuomintang resisted the Japanese seizure of Shanghai in February 1932 the Chinese Communists quite naturally continued to call on the people "to arm themselves to topple the Kuomintang, which is surrendering and selling out the nation to the imperialists". The people were instructed to "unfold the national revolutionary war under the leadership of the Soviet Government to oppose the Japanese and all other imperialists, to win the independence and liberation of the Chinese nation!".[9] At one and the same time Communists were expected to fight on two fronts – against their potential allies and against the foreign enemy. The Shanghai incident illustrates the chaos this engendered. Faced with the task of opposing all and sundry, local Party cells chose their own priorities. In reaction to this anarchy, in mid-February the Central Committee despatched a "Directive to Local Party Offices About the Shanghai Incident", criticising two "extremes", both of which were said to be "intolerable". Firstly there was the "closed-door" attitude: not letting Communists participate in the anti-imperialist movement. Its counterpart – the completely "open-door" attitude – resulted in the Party becoming "captive to the Kuomintang". Worse forms of disorientation were evident. The Shensi Provincial Committee, in particular, came under attack for shifting "from one extreme to the other". First it adopted a "negative, closed-door attitude towards the anti-Japanese movement". Then it took the opposite line. The Szechwan Provincial Committee was not much better, as the Directive pointed out:

> When the broad masses rose up against the Japanese, they advocated 'opposition to the imperialists', not to the Japanese. They went to the other extreme after finding out their mistake, and organized the 'Committee for the Support of General Ma Chan-shan', and demanded protection by the Kuomintang Government. They even openly indicated in their publications a wish to co-operate with the Kuomintang.

Elsewhere, in Manchuria and Kwantung, the latter tendency was also said to be in evidence.[10] On the other side of the picture were those provincial committees, as in Honan, which ignored the issue of fighting the imperialists altogether.[11] The Kiangsu Committee, which did make some moves in this direction, was accused of mere "window-dressing".[12]

Undoubtedly much of this confusion can be attributed to the contradictory demands placed on the CCP at all levels since the previous September, arising from both Chiang Kai-shek's unrelenting hostility at the helm of the Kuomintang and the Japanese invasion itself. But in Moscow too, the Comintern was caught in a tangle, attempting to reconcile the conflicting demands of Soviet realpolitik and the sectarian demands on sections imposed at the VI Congress in 1928. The first clear sign that the fog might be lifting did not appear until March 1932, with an article by Wang Ming, China's representative on the Comintern executive committee. Poised awkwardly between the demands of the Soviet state and the interests of the Chinese revolution (as interpreted in the light of the VI Congress), Wang stressed the importance of the anti-Japanese resistance. Japanese imperialism was an immediate threat to both the Chinese revolution and the USSR, he argued, adding that:

> Under the prevailing conditions of open armed intervention by imperialism, the massed millions of China have faced a dilemma: either once and for all become the colonial slaves of Japanese, English, American and French imperialism, or rise up in direct armed struggle for the independence and liberation of China.

However, this was a shift in emphasis rather than a total alteration of purpose. Wang still insisted that the revolutionary war "against the imperialists and the Kuomintang" was to be treated as one war,[13] and we know, from evidence of his hostility towards united front policies in the mid-thirties, that Wang needed little persuasion to recommend this course to his comrades in China.[14]

The rest of the Communist movement was also called to arms. Barely a week after the Japanese attack on Manchuria, Dimitrov, then heading the Comintern's West European Bureau in Berlin, took the initiative and sent the following message to the executive in Moscow:

> In connection with Japan's military operations in Manchuria the war danger has directly intensified, for these may develop into an attack on the Soviet Union which has long been in preparation. We consider it to be absolutely necessary, therefore, that our parties should step up the campaign against the war danger and in defence of the Soviet Union.[15]

But the Comintern was extremely slow to react. Dimitrov's warnings did not find an echo until the beginning of November when *l'Humanité* published an appeal from the International Committee for the Defence of Chinese Workers and Peasants (a Communist front organisation). It warned that the Far Eastern conflict might lead to a world war and that the Japanese were "preparing to attack the Soviet Union", calling on all China aid committees to broaden their activities by organising meetings and demonstrations of protest against Japanese aggression.[16] This summons was then repeated by the British, Spanish, Polish and French Communist Parties into the New Year.[17]

Having been itself slow to respond to the emergency at the outset, the Comintern secretariat now harshly reprimanded member sections for their inactivity. *Kommunisticheskii Internatsional* published the following criticism of foreign parties on the 10 December 1931:

> Even when Japanese guns thundered in the immediate neighbourhood of the Soviet Union, many comrades failed to understand the intimate connexion between the Japanese attack on Manchuria and the preparation of a great anti-Soviet war. This obliges us again and again to focus the attention of all Communist Parties and the whole of the international proletariat on this burning question.

The writer went on to criticise "individual Parties or Party members" for overestimating the conflicts amongst the USSR's rivals and underestimating those between Moscow and the capitalist world. He called on all Communist Parties to create a greater "united front from below" against the imperialist Powers and "against the partition of China".[18] This was followed at the end of the month by Wang Ming's exhortation, directed above all at the Japanese, American, British and French Communist Parties, to prevent the transportation of arms and men to China.[19]

From propaganda to action: the Comintern now became increasingly strident in its exhortations to sabotage the shipment of armaments to Japan:

> At this hour [February 1932] all Communist Parties must once again turn to the workers of all countries with the call: Whether or not the European countries cause the whole globe to slide into world war depends on you and your activity against the war that has broken out. Act, act, act!

Furthermore, action meant going one step beyond the wide-spread system of observing and reporting the movement of armaments and ammunition. It also meant strikes:

> *Decisive mobilisation of the masses* is required, primarily against the transportation of weapons and military supplies, which travel to Japan along the tracks of every capitalist railway and from the ports of every capitalist country.[20]

Yet Communists abroad still failed to recognise "that the defence of the national and territorial integrity of China is an inseparable constituent part of the defence of the USSR, of the Chinese soviets, of the defence of the whole world proletariat from imperialist war". This was particularly true of countries on the periphery of world politics, like Czechoslovakia, Norway and Sweden, which none the less played a significant role in supplying Japan with war material, through either manufacture or transportation.[21]

A special responsibility lay with the French, British, American, German, Czech, Polish and Romanian Communist Parties who were charged with the task of "preventing the transportation of military supplies destined for use against China and the USSR, by all available means of mass action by workers and peasants". Hitherto all that had occurred were "the passing of resolutions and at best the arranging of meetings and relatively modest demonstrations". What action was envisaged?:

> What is required above all is mass action: 1) strikes in the factories working for defence and in enterprises involved in transportation: all-out strikes, partial strikes – in individual shops, lengthy, short-term, Italian [factory occupation], etc.; 2) protest demonstrations; 3) as to Japanese emissaries with the impudence to ensure the fulfilment of orders for their war of plunder openly in front of the workers – throw them unceremoniously out of the factories; 4) mass action to prevent the transportation of military supplies; 5) the organisation of revolutionary action by soldiers, sailors and recruits, and so on and so forth.[22]

Communist Parties were severely castigated for their insensibility to the dangers that the Russians faced, without being told exactly why there was the need for so much urgency. In March 1932 Moscow vented its wrath once more:

> Military cargo reaches its destination without hindrance, even though the weapons and other military material are being produced and transported by *workers*.

Communists were indulging in "empty phrases" about decisive action "*when* the imperialists dare to attack the USSR":

> If it is not explained to the masses all the time that not today, not now, but later, the time will come for decisive action to defend the USSR; if the beginning of intervention is illustrated in terms of a sudden, unrepeated act on the USSR's Western frontier, and the struggle against intervention as a similarly sudden and unrepeated action; then when "war breaks out", the masses, as a result of this kind of indoctrination, may only have the impression that "for the moment it is still unimportant", and when it develops further "then we'll cope with it".

The problem of apathy was apparently not unrelated to the fact that, whereas it was easier to rally workers to the direct defence of the USSR, it was another matter where China was concerned. As the Comintern complained:

> It is asserted that the masses will act decisively as soon as it is a matter of intervention against the USSR, but it is not possible to rouse them to active support for the Chinese, even in the form of refusing to produce or transport weapons.[23]

New tactics had to be tried.

But it evidently took a good deal of persuasion for the Russians to accept that Communist Parties should broaden the anti-war movement to encompass more than class-conscious militants by appealing also to "bourgeois pacifists" – the same constituency which the Soviet Government was attempting to sway through its disarmament campaign. As far as one can see, Moscow had hitherto sanctioned only one such appeal: the declaration from an international committee for the defence of the Soviet Union against imperialist warmongers, on the 11 December 1930.

Signed by Maxim Gorky, Upton Sinclair, Henri Barbusse and Willi Münzenberg, this was the latter's creation. An entrepreneurial and highly unorthodox German Communist, he directed the appeal not merely at "workers, peasants, toilers", but also at "sympathetic intellectuals and representatives of the petty bourgeois strata", its purpose being to campaign against war and in defence of the USSR.[24] Although the committee had no formal ties with the Comintern, its pursuit of the pacifist lobby in the West was still regarded as dangerously heretical by the sectarian element which dominated world Communism at that time. For it was strongly felt that, whilst the Soviet Government proper could appeal to bourgeois pacifism, the Comintern and its sections should be prohibited from pandering to such perilous tendencies. As it was, Soviet disarmament propaganda at Geneva co-existed extremely uneasily with the Comintern's anti-pacifist sentiments; both had to be kept in quarantine from one another.

This point of view was vigorously defended in an article by "Al'fred", entitled "On the Inopportune Application of the Peace Slogan", which appeared in print on the 10 May 1932. With a liberal sprinkling of quotations from Lenin, the author roundly condemned the purely pacifist propaganda put about by leading Communist Parties – notably the PCF, working in a country where militarism had engendered a strongly pacifist response. They were now reminded that the main issue was not "peace":

> It is apparent that Communists in France and Germany can not call for the maintenance of the current imperialist 'peace', for this would mean giving their blessing to the Versailles robbers' peace and making peace with that state of affairs which predominates under the capitalist 'peace', making peace with that crisis and ghastly condition of the toiling masses, from which they are seeking a way out in revolution. Certainly there can be no question about all this. Consequently there can also be no question about the correctness of the peace slogan given the existing state of affairs in Western Europe in the sense of maintaining the current 'peace'.

Behind this reasoning lay a recognition of the USSR's continued need to maintain discord within the capitalist camp, but at the same time a real concern lest pacifism debilitate the fighting spirit of the working classes — the assumption being that the road to power would most probably go by way of armed struggle. As Al'fred pointed out, in criticising a German Communist for lapsing into pacifist propaganda:

> Of course there is nothing bad in succeeding, through some means or other, in deceiving the class enemy. But the trouble is that by such manoeuvres the enemy is not outwitted and one may cause considerable bewilderment amongst one's own ranks.

The KPD had actually printed an article which suggested that Litvinov's speech to the Geneva disarmament conference serve as "a programme for the leadership of the struggle of the entire working class from peace".[25] In drawing a clear distinction between Comintern and Soviet governmental policies, Al'fred had to become rather more explicit about the aims behind Moscow's stand at Geneva than Litvinov would have liked:

> At Geneva comrade Litvinov represented the Soviet Government, and standing at its rear the toiling masses of the Soviet Union. The value of his speech for the struggle of the working class of capitalist countries lies in the fact that yet again it emphasises the reluctance of the imperialists to disarm and once more assures everyone of the sincerity of the Soviet Union's peace policy and the need to defend it by every means.

Thus in supporting the USSR's peace policy, Communists in the West were instructed "not to mechanically transfer the Soviet Union's peace policy slogans into conditions of class struggle within capitalist countries".[26]

This article by no means signified the final word on the matter for, as the editor of *Kommunisticheskii Internatsional* pointed out, its publication did "not settle the question". It appears, instead, to have represented a parting shot from those who had lost a battle in the upper reaches of the Communist movement. The victor was Münzenberg, whose proposals[27] for a world anti-war congress had been accepted by the Comintern executive's political commission on the 27 April 1932, with the vital condition that the committee set up to prepare the congress should have a broad non-party character.[28] The prominent French littérateurs, Henri Barbusse and Romain Rolland, were used as figureheads to give the affair an air of bourgeois respectability,[29] and invitations were issued in their name stressing that "they represented no particular political party and ... had no organisation".[30] When it convened in Amsterdam from the 27 to the 29 August 1932, it represented an assembly of 2 200 delegates from some 27 different countries.

However, there could have been few illusions that this experiment would prove an easy task, for the militancy of the Communists present jarred with the pacifism expressed by many delegates, and its organisers were naturally more concerned about the dangers of war for the Soviet Union, particularly from Japan, rather than the ethics of war in general. He who receives the bullet is braver than he who fires the gun, argued Patel, representing Gandhi's movement, to which Münzenberg caustically responded: "Maybe, but it's a fact that he who fires the bullet stays upright, while he who receives it falls to the ground."[31] Indeed, the whole congress had opened in an atmosphere of unreality. The first day was almost entirely expended in the broadcasting of fraternal greetings, which left Münzenberg, for one, totally exasperated. Thus when his turn to speak arrived, he spent his time attacking the other delegates. Speeches by Gorky and Shvernik (the Soviet trade union leader), which were delivered in their absence since the Dutch refused them entry, were scarcely more positive in tone. For what the Communists really wanted was to mobilise pacifist elements into halting the flow of munitions to Japan. Sen Katayama, representing the Japanese Communist Party on the Comintern executive, reached the heart of the matter, pleading with the delegates:

> I know how hard it is for those who are starving and unemployed to refuse to load and transport arms and munitions for Japan, but don't forget that you, by handling such shipments, are helping to murder your fellow workers and to attack the Soviet Union, which is the guarantee of your hope for socialism.

Given the distinctly ethereal nature of the proceedings, the resultant manifesto comes as some surprise; but then the Comintern's men had not been idle behind the scenes. The manifesto squared neatly with the demands of Soviet foreign policy, denouncing imperialism and asserting that "a definite armed crusade against the Soviet Union" was "being openly prepared in the Far East". It strongly repudiated the "legend of 'red imperialism'", indicating that there had been some dissent over the adoption of this pro-Soviet line. Opposition to the Versailles treaty was also expressed, alongside a condemnation of "the leading role played by French imperialism". Even on the issue of pacifism, the manifesto succeeded in harmonising with Moscow's opinions.[32] A vivid illustration of this came with *Pravda*'s publication of the manifesto. Although minor but revealing alterations appeared in the text, in every other respect it was published in full.[33] Münzenberg's tactics were thus vindicated, though the argument that little of a concrete nature had actually been achieved could scarcely be rejected.

*   *   *

The official counterpart to the campaign against war was the Soviet Government's pursuit of disarmament. Yet the contrast between the feverish preparations for war in the Far East taking place in the Soviet Union and the tragically vacuous discussions at Geneva about disarming for peace could hardly have been more blatant. Even so, the fact that the Soviets not only chose to conceal these war preparations from the public but also decided to attend the world disarmament conference when it opened in February 1932 neatly illustrates the philosophy underlying Litvinov's foreign policy.

The Russians had openly derided the results of the League preparatory commission on disarmament. One authoritative Soviet commentator, probably Boris Shtein, head of the Narkomindel's Central European department and a known associate of Litvinov, reasserted a fundamentalist Leninist position when he wrote that it is "laughable to think and expect that any of the imperialist states is seriously thinking about a reduction in armaments".[34] At the same time, however, and this could not be said so openly, the Russians – and Litvinov in particular – were looking to widen any chink in the armour of capitalism. Thus attendance at Geneva was less a luxury than a necessity. It would also appear that not all in Moscow were equally pessimistic, as the Soviet Government's declaration to the Powers in January 1931 indicates; for it included the statement that "the question of prolonging and strengthening peace or of a new destructive war might depend to a significant extent on the results of the conference".[35] This pragmatism was rooted in Litvinov's temperament. He consistently and obstinately refused to see world politics in terms of certainties or as a mere machine with economic forces as the mainspring. His force of personality and Stalin's acquiescence ensured that this view prevailed, though the extreme tetchiness which imbued Moscow's correspondence with the League Secretary-General testified to continued unease at acceptance of compromise.[36] What ultimately drove the Russians to Geneva was the compelling fear that their very absence would only facilitate anti-Soviet machinations – when they were not present they always sensed themselves to be the object of the conversation – and the Japanese attack on Manchuria, whilst it ripped the tattered veil of conviction from the whole enterprise, simultaneously reinforced the USSR's determination to avoid exclusion and isolation in the world arena at all costs.

The Russians were, in fact, in an extremely awkward position. As a result of the threat from Japan, they had to rearm themselves sufficiently to deter this potential aggressor; on the other hand, they could not afford to alienate the other Powers who were broaching the issue of disarmament, however spuriously. They therefore trod warily at Geneva, paying ritualistic observance at the altar of disarmament, whilst simultaneously distancing themselves from League involvement in the Manchurian crisis.[37] On the 9 September 1931, the Italians had put forward proposals for "a real and effective truce in armaments" until the disarmament conference had met and finished its business.[38] These proposals looked distinctly unreal after the Japanese launched their assault on Manchuria nine days later. Nonetheless, when pressed, Moscow publicly welcomed the idea of a moratorium, provided "all countries" accepted it with respect to "all types of armaments".[39] The Soviet position was further complicated when the League then passed a resolution on the 29 September, bringing the armaments truce into effect from the beginning of November.[40] But the danger of isolation receded when the British made clear that they too would only adhere on specific conditions – reserving the right to withdraw in the event of an attack on any of their possessions. Clearly the Russians were not alone in their anxieties about Japanese intentions.

However, the conference itself was bound to place the Russians in a quandary. The Western Powers felt obliged to make some progress in disarmament, if only to appease a vociferous section of public opinion. On the other hand, it was unlikely that such measures would in any way go far enough to relieve the Russians of their anxieties about defence against Japan. It was at the same time vital to stress the USSR's interest in peaceful co-existence with the capitalist Powers. The conference finally met on the 2 February 1932 against the unsettling background of war in China. Litvinov unrestrained in his invective and repeated his customary call for general and complete disarmament, still immaculate in its pristine impracticability. But this was mere rhetoric on his part. He also took seriously the need to appear flexible, stressing his delegation's willingness to "discuss any proposal in the direction of reducing armaments".[41] But by now his masters had no real interest in the idea. Litvinov was wedged in between French attempts to provoke the Russians into "voting against decisions unanimously accepted by other delegates",[42] and Moscow's need to pursue rearmament unimpeded by international obligations.[43] This unenviable dilemma was resolved to Litvinov's disadvantage. When, five months later, the conference at last adopted a resolution on the absolute prohibition of air attack on civilian populations (scarcely of concern to the Russians given the distances separating them from hostile air bases) and of chemical, bacteriological and incendiary warfare (duplicating the 1925 Geneva Protocol), the Soviet delegation was instructed to vote against it, which left the Russians in the somewhat dubious company of the Germans, who openly sought rearmament.[44] This represented a defeat for Litvinov's line, not because he believed such measures were of any real use, but because it left the Russians isolated at Geneva. In fact the USSR's position at this time was typified more by the attempts of Radek to recruit Liddell Hart as an adviser to the Red Army on mechanised warfare – though this was probably an example of his impish sense of humour – than Litvinov's verbal acrobatics at the conference itself.[45] Those in Moscow who had always viewed Geneva with distaste did not hide their contempt. "The conference on disarmament which has just taken place in Geneva vividly and irrefutably shows in practice the impossibility of any kind of disarmament whatever in capitalist conditions", commented the Comintern journal, burying the corpse with undisguised satisfaction.[46]

9 The Impact of the Far Eastern Crisis upon Soviet Policy in Europe: 1932

The main link between the Far Eastern crisis and events in Europe was the problem of France. The French Government had, indeed, initialled a non-aggression pact with the USSR in the summer of 1931, but it had then refused to progress any further. Soviet diplomats spoke in private of the French move as merely "a manoeuvre" prompted temporarily by the crisis over the Austro-German customs union.[1] In the Soviet press Paris was still stigmatised as *"one of the most important centres of European reaction"*.[2] Existing suspicions about French intentions had been deepened by Laval's attempts to secure a rapprochement with Germany at Soviet expense, and on top of this came the Manchurian crisis and simultaneous evidence of French support of Japan.

The French had their own interests to protect in the Far East – not only "concessions" in China, which were already under the shadow of Japanese expansion, but also the colony of Indochina, where demands for the boycott of Japanese goods made them increasingly nervous about the possibility of a backlash from Tokyo.[3] Their policy was dictated by the fact that they were incapable of defending these possessions against external attack and were therefore determined that, in the event of French mediation failing, the Japanese should not actively be discouraged from heading further north, rather than southwards.[4] This much became apparent to the Russians barely a month after the Japanese occupied Manchuria. At the outset France held the League presidency and attempted to use its good offices to resolve the Sino-Japanese conflict. As a Quai official noted: "Since the onset of the current crisis in the Far East, the French Government has, in its unceasing efforts at the League of

97

Nations as in the field of diplomacy, constantly set its sights on the re-establishment of normal relations between China and Japan."[5] This in itself was sufficient to arouse anxieties in Moscow, let alone when viewed in the light of French press speculation hinting at collusion between Paris and Tokyo. The Russians therefore prompted the French Communist Party into action. On the 30 October 1931 PCF Deputies addressed a letter to Foreign Minister Briand, pointing in an accusatory manner to his attempts at a growing number of "secret meetings" in Geneva to "regulate inter-imperialist disagreements" over what was euphemistically termed "Japanese intervention". The letter went on to remark that "certain newspapers close to government circles have no hesitation in engaging in anti-Soviet provocations by writing that 'Japan alone is capable of bringing down the formidable power of the Soviet Union' and that the steppes of Siberia could one day become the battlefield on which 'Bolshevism' will meet its end".[6]

It is easy to dismiss such Soviet fears as unnecessarily alarmist, but one must recall that the Russians were not alone in harbouring these suspicions. Western newspaper reports early in 1932 of a secret Franco-Japanese agreement elicited anxious enquiries from the US Secretary of State to the French Government, though the Americans were more receptive to the subsequent denials than were the Russians.[7] In Paris the Soviet embassy received reports from "a source of known reliability" that, to escape being pilloried for offering the Japanese Government credit guarantees for arms purchases, the French Government had accepted the firm Mitsubishi as a fictitious buyer, thus enabling the Japanese to obtain security for 800 million francs worth of munitions.[8] Furthermore, when negotiating the Franco-Soviet non-aggression pact in August 1932 the French Government attempted to insert a clause in the draft agreement stipulating its abrogation in the event of "an attack on a third Power" (a reference to Japan in all but name),[9] and one month later it advised the Japanese against signing a similar pact with the Soviet Union[10] – difficult to explain except in terms of a French attempt to turn Japanese forces northwards. As a consequence Soviet commentators spoke of a "new military alliance of the two most militaristic and aggressive countries in the world"; others were more cautious, arguing that "*co-operation between Japan and France*"[11] was "a fact" yet adding that "whether there exists between them a formal alliance or not, we do not know, but this is not the decisive question anyway".[12]

Soviet unease at the supposed extent of collusion between France and Japan only heightened anxieties longstanding in Moscow that Berlin and Paris would come to terms. Laval certainly aimed at a rapprochement with Germany. This was closely linked in his own mind with the removal of all Soviet influence from Central Europe. As the British ambassador to Paris rightly noted: "He believes bolshevism to constitute a menace to our civilisation unless the present chaotic state of international production and marketing (industrial and agricultural) is remedied. This conviction is the basis of his policy towards Germany. One outcome of it is the establishment of the Franco-German Committee, the task of which is to organise the industrial production and marketing of the two countries as a first step towards the essential coordination of the economic activity of Europe as a whole. Another manifestation of this conviction is his desire to turn Germany from Russia which has, I understand, already met with some response in Berlin".[13] Yet Brüning's visit to Paris had been unsuccessful, though Laval continued undeterred in pursuit of his elusive goal. To this end he secured the appointment of his under-secretary of state as ambassador to Berlin from the 21 September. André Francois-Poncet was chosen as a known Germanophile with no previous experience of diplomacy. He arrived in Berlin "with the idea that a rapprochement with Germany, if it had run aground thanks to the Left, could eventually be made to succeed by the Right".[14] This was followed by the arrival of Briand and Laval in the German capital on the 27 September and although these negotiations proved as fruitless as before – Laval's hands were by now tied by the prospect of forthcoming elections in France – the French Premier continued to meet with the German ambassador to Paris in an effort to find common ground on reparations.

In this atmosphere of continuing uncertainty the Russians could do little but bank upon "not only the exacerbation of contradictions between the imperialists of France, England, the USA", but also "well-known clashes within the camp of the German bourgeoisie".[15] *Pravda* was talking in terms of a split between, on the one hand, the National Party and the NSDAP, and on the other "a well-known group of German bankers" who sought "an agreement with French imperialism" with the aid of "the German social-Fascists" (the SPD). "An 'agreement' with France, given the current balance of power between the French and German bourgeoisie, would essentially amount to *surrender by the German bourgeoisie to French imperialism*", warned the Soviet press in January 1932.[16] Thus the KPD was in no circumstances permitted to give way to what the Soviets referred to as "*the manoeuvres of German social-Fascism*", when the SPD called for a united front at all levels against the Nazis.[17] In this Moscow was not injecting an alien philosophy into the ranks of the KPD. It was rather a matter of reinforcing the more extremist elements within the Party who, at the Presidential elections in April 1932, argued "in favour of voting for Hitler on the principle that the greater the Nazi vote, the greater would be the unrest in Germany and in Europe".[18] Although KPD leader Thälmann condemned such views as "*very dangerous for the proletariat*",[19] they nonetheless continued as a strong undercurrent in the Party's ranks, for they did at least match the hidden logic of Moscow's policy. What this amounted to was an unholy and unforeseen alliance between Soviet realpolitik and Comintern revolutionary extremism, emerging from a common but independently conceived hostility towards the stabilisation of Europe.

This bond proved exceptionally difficult to break. Even what *Pravda* correctly acknowledged to be "the massive growth in the number of electors voting for the Fascist National-Socialist Party" at the Prussian Landtag elections in April 1932 was resolutely subordinated to the overriding consideration that this spelt a decisive fall in SPD support, due to "a growth in dissatisfaction amongst the broadest masses with the policy of submission to the dictates of France".[20] It is at this stage important to reiterate that the negligible attention paid towards the NSDAP (relative to the Socialists) was rooted in a complacent assessment of the Party's coherence and the quality of its leadership, and that this colossal misjudgement was as common elsewhere in Europe as it was in Moscow. Unfortunately for the Soviets, those whom they most trusted in Berlin – the military – were equally prone to be contemptuous of Hitler, as will become evident. The following comment from General von Hammerstein, commander of the Reichswehr, to the British ambassador was typical of the reassurances given to the Russians: "it was absurd to compare Hitler with Mussolini. Hitler was in reality a very mediocre personality".[21] This was precisely what Stalin and his colleagues wished to hear.

It would, however, be wrong to suppose that these treasured assumptions went unchallenged in Moscow. There were dissenting voices within the KPD and the Comintern, who argued, albeit quietly, for a common front with the Social Democrats and who were accordingly vilified as "opportunists".[22] Similarly, the lack of consensus within the Narkomindel during the summer of 1931 over the significance of the NSDAP also re-emerged in the spring of 1932, as Nazi electoral successes once again brought this issue to the forefront of attention. The following is from a letter from Khinchuk, polpred in Berlin, to Deputy Commissar Krestinsky – who in 1931, at least, shared in the prevailing sense of complacency about the Nazis – dated the 28 April 1932:

> The results of the elections show a tendency for the Fascist camp, and above all the 'Nazis', to grow stronger, From 1928 we have seen a deafening growth of the 'Nazis', and a sudden change is at present difficult to foresee. ... what is noticeable is a growing tendency for the 'Nazis' to steal their way to power, and sooner or later they may succeed. Therefore one cannot but pay attention to likely changes in the political arena. The information which has reached us in the form of comments from journalists and soundings of our own may turn out to be incorrect. As you know, we have no direct contacts with the 'Nazis'. Nevertheless, Hitler's interview with foreign correspondents[23] is impossible to ignore. In this interview and in innumerable speeches Hitler specifically states that his task is to fight the USSR. Germany is not Italy, and Hitler is not Mussolini. I am pointing this out, not with a view to sowing panic, but only to point to the need to study in greater depth and explore further the movement actually here, in order to have the possibility of correctly evaluating every factor in Germany.[24]

As the apologetic tone of the letter indicates, Khinchuk was preaching to sceptics. In the confusion surrounding policy towards Germany, at least one section of the Soviet apparatus was taking the Nazi threat seriously,[25] but the prevailing mood was still one of excessive complacency, the wish being father to the thought. Events in both the summer and autumn of 1932 only reinforced this attitude.

The collapse of Laval's government in February had not entirely ended French attempts at a reconciliation with Germany. Although his successor Tardieu was no Germanophile, he was also strongly anti-Soviet, and under his Government others continued in the search for a modus vivendi with Germany, albeit with only semi-official blessing. In Berlin François-Poncet pursued that end with as much if not more ingenuity as before.[26] In Luxembourg a group of French, Belgian and German industrialists and bankers gathered under the auspices of the Franco-German Information and Documentation Committee (CFAID) from the 29 to the 30 April, united by a common fear of Bolshevism and determined to further the resolution of their countries' political differences through economic and financial co-operation.[27] These activities had no direct results, but they undoubtedly lent credence to the belief that an initiative in this direction would fall on fertile ground in France. On the 1 June the Brüning Government finally collapsed. The incoming administration was headed by von Papen, a maverick figure within the Centre Party, representing the Catholic Right and, more importantly, a prominent advocate of reconciliation with France at Soviet expense. Aware of Papen's views and hypersensitive to rumours of Franco-German collaboration, the Russians once more sought consolation in the countervailing power of resurgent nationalism in Germany. "The new German Government has also to take into account the nationalist wave which has arisen . . . as a result of the increasingly burdensome yoke of the Versailles system, and which has drawn many millions of the urban petty bourgeoisie, peasants and even individual workers into Hitler's camp", *Pravda* reassured its readers, adding that: "These millions voted in the Presidential and Prussian elections not so much for Hitler, as against France and Poland".[28]

Soviet reliance on the "nationalist wave" grew rather than lessened when it became evident that von Papen was not merely receptive to French advances, unlikely now that Herriot had succeeded Tardieu as Premier on the 3 June. He was also prepared to initiate action himself. It was therefore unfortunate, to say the least, that Khinchuk played down the dangers von Papen represented in order to dramatise the threat from Hitler, for this undoubtedly weakened his credibility in Moscow. He wrote to Krestinsky on the 25 June arguing that: "The Papen Government up to now has not taken any steps or made any official statements testifying to the fact that it will adopt a more hostile stand towards the USSR than did the Brüning Government." He then went on to claim that Hitler, on the other hand, was an entirely different matter:

> there have already been anti-Soviet demands and decla-rations on the part of the National Socialists, on whom the present government depends, and who will, in one form or another, exert great influence on Government policy in the immediate future.
>
> The National Socialists offer no outline of their political stance in relation to the USSR, and give the impression that in this instance their silence is intentional. Thus, in a book which the National Socialists brought out in May, issues relating to Eastern policy were discussed, but the USSR was passed over. In the introduction Rosenberg, in outlining the principles behind the National Socialists' Eastern policy, has merely said that the USSR is a special case. Professor Herliand's demand that the *Bersenzeitung* and the National Socialists speak out on their position vis-à-vis an Eastern or Western orientation and dispel 'Moscow's anxiety', has been left unanswered by the National Socialists. But, in keeping silent on the issue of the principles behind their general position, the National Socialists are with growing ferocity attacking current trade policy towards the USSR.

These attacks included a speech by Gregor Strasser to the Reichstag and articles in the Nazi newspaper *Angriff* on the 17 and 22 June. In Khinchuk's opinion this was "symptomatic of the line held by the National Socialists in relation to the USSR".[29]

The news reaching Moscow very soon after this letter arrived will have reinforced existing doubts about Khinchuk's good judgement. It was by the end of June an open secret that on the 16th of that month von Papen had offered the French what amounted to an entente at Soviet expense.[30] This took place at Lausanne, where the Great Powers had convened a meeting to resolve the reparations issue. News of the offer became public, evidently as a result of French indiscretions. A report on the subject appeared in *Pravda* on the 1 July.[31] In fact it all amounted to little more than a crude attempt at manoeuvring the French into an acceptance of German rearmament by building on their fear of Bolshevism. In making this move von Papen had seriously overestimated the extent to which these fears would distract the French from the dangers of a revanchist Germany. This and further offers of a similar nature were diplomatically brushed aside.[32]

Papen's moves proved more significant for Soviet policy than for the French.[33] They undermined Khinchuk in his warnings against the Nazi menace and blinded Stalin and his colleagues to the threat from that quarter. Further confirmation that fears of Hitler were misplaced came from conversations with the German military. On the 27 June War Minister von Schleicher told Khinchuk that "the National Socialists also favour maintaining relations with the USSR. True, they stand for a desperate struggle and a close fight with domestic Communists, but this can not have any connexion with the USSR".[34] And, true to form, the Soviet press expressed its satisfaction that "resistance" to the Papen proposals came "even from within the camp of the German bourgeoisie".[35]

A curious pattern emerges. When the Communists in Germany appear to be weak – as in the spring elections and on the 20 July when Papen's seizure of power in Prussia found the KPD incapable of organising any resistance, even a general strike[36] – the Russians rely increasingly on the "nationalist wave" in Germany; and when the Communists become stronger, and the Nazis weaker – as happens during the autumn of 1932 – it becomes less important to rely on the nationalists, but at the same time and by the same token it also rules them out as a serious potential threat. This was not merely a natural response to the apparent logic of the situation. It was also the product of a long-held belief in the beneficial effects of German nationalism for Soviet security; the Rapallo tradition took as long to die in the USSR as it did in Germany, as events from 1933 to 1939 were to demonstrate.

German nationalism did not merely act as a restraint on France. It also impelled the Poles to seek a rapprochement with the USSR, and at a time when Japan's expansion into Manchuria accentuated existing Soviet concern to settle relations by finalising a non-aggression pact. According to Radek, "Stalin feared a simultaneous Japanese–Polish attack,"[37] and when Polish

President Pilsudski visited Bucharest in April 1932, the Narkomindel speculated pessimistically as to whether he intended to hold "concrete military discussions in case of war betwen Poland, Romania and the Soviet Union in connexion with Far Eastern complications".[38] In fact the President appears to have gone to coax the Romanians into an accommodation with Moscow as part of his strategy of coordinating all Baltic and East European negotiations with the USSR, the aim being to secure a Soviet commitment to non-aggression with respect to all these states prior to the conclusion of a Polish-Soviet pact.[39] Finland settled with Moscow in January,[40] Latvia in February[41] and Estonia in May[42]; Lithuania, still technically at war with Poland and therefore reliant upon Soviet good-will, had come to terms in May 1931.[43]

Soviet diplomats may have incorrectly assessed Pilsudski's visit to Bucharest, but they were right in assuming that Poland was unlikely to contemplate any immediate aggression against the USSR, for the Polish Government's own international position was uncertain; as Stomonyakov at the Narkomindel acknowledged: "Poland ... must first know whom it will have to deal with tomorrow in Germany and France: with Brüning or Hitler, with Tardieu or the French Radicals, who are fairly cool about the alliance with Poland".[44] It was this sense of uncertainty that finally drove the Poles into concluding a non-aggression pact with Moscow on the 25 July, having given up hope of persuading the Romanians to act in concert.[45] Not only had the Radicals come to power in France, but the feverish campaign for the Reichstag elections by the extreme Right silenced any doubts about the menace threatening from Germany. Although initial Soviet press comment on the pact was tactful on this point,[46] Radek's analysis was characteristically less inhibited:

> The Polish Fascist Government, *faced with growing German nationalism*, fears that in the event of a crisis leading to war, the French petty bourgeois masses may force their government to forego Poland. Therefore the Polish Fascists, having for a number of years proclaimed a crusade against the USSR, *are attempting to strengthen their position both in relation to Germany and in relation to French imperialism by concluding a pact with the USSR.* They are demonstrating that in the event of surprises on the part of an indecisive French ally, then

Poland will be able to concentrate all its forces in defence of its territory from the West.[47]

Thus whilst the conclusion of this pact marked a significant improvement in the USSR's international position, lessening the likelihood of a war on two fronts and paving the way for a final settlement with France, it also further strengthened the argument that German nationalism was now paying dividends, of which the Polish pact was only one of the first.

10 A Temporary Setback in Relations with Britain

The conclusion of the Polish-Soviet non-aggression pact augured well for Moscow's future. The Soviet Union at last appeared to be harvesting international rewards for the desperate sacrifices of the previous three years. A series of further successes, both real and apparent, in the autumn and winter of 1932 – both within Germany and elsewhere – appeared firm confirmation that the USSR had finally established itself as a Power to be reckoned with. The only setback occurred in relations with Britain, yet even this proved shortlived and seemed only to underline the progress Moscow had made.

The collapse of Labour and the advent of a national coalition under MacDonald in August 1931 had failed to occasion much concern in the USSR, once it was understood that the dreaded Churchill would have no part in the new administration.[1] Admittedly, the mutiny of naval ratings at Invergordon on the 15 September excited some interest amongst hotheads at the Comintern,[2] but the British Communist Party's enduring impotence[3], and the great loss of support for Labour at elections on the 27 October, shattered any remaining illusions. As Comintern secretary Kuusinen remarked from his vantage point at the head of the section for Anglo-Saxon countries: "Say what you like about the English bourgeoisie, but one thing that is impossible to deny is that it knows how to manoeuvre in politics."[4] Others less directly concerned with the world revolutionary process drew more fundamental conclusions. For example Voroshilov "did not appear to think that countries with 'an old culture' such as Great Britain would ever have anything in the nature of a bolshevik revolution".[5] This left the Russians at the mercy of the British Conservative Party and it was not long before its traditional hostility – constantly fuelled by Comintern agitation in the empire – found a timely ally in the new spirit of protectionism at home and in the Dominions overseas.

As usual Britain's trade with the USSR was a ready target. It had, in fact, never fully recovered from the embargo Moscow imposed after London broke off relations in 1927, and the Russians could always obtain more favourable terms of credit in Germany. Thus the British faced a passive balance of trade, leaving some £25 millions to Moscow's advantage in 1930. This was to some extent offset by British earnings from 'invisibles' (banking, insurance, shipping), but not sufficiently to deprive the anti-Soviet lobby of a plausible grievance, which they pressed home vociferously under Labour.[6] Action was therefore only to be expected when the Conservatives entered the new coalition in the summer of 1931. With the Import Duties Bill laid before Parliament early in February 1932,[7] the new Foreign Secretary, Sir John Simon – formerly a Liberal – warned the Soviet chargé d'affaires, Bogomolov, that the trade gap with his country had to be closed. Were nothing done, "Parliamentary and public criticism ... would certainly arise very shortly", and the British Government would then have to "consider seriously the question of taking steps to attain the ends desired".[8]

Preoccupied with more pressing matters elsewhere, Moscow responded with indifference, evidently in the belief that London could contemplate no measures which might risk a further loss in existing trade and, also, no doubt, due to Soviet difficulties in financing current imports, let alone an increase merely to appease the British.[9] But all the British Government needed to prompt it into action was additional pressure from outside. Canada obliged. The wave of protectionism beating on British shores was also evident across the Atlantic, and, like the USA, Canada was a direct competitor with Russia in the exportation of primary produce. Thus, when the British and the Dominions met at Ottawa in late July 1932 to settle the issue of reciprocal imperial preferences, the Canadian Premier, Bennett, a tough conservative, made the solution of the Russian question the precondition of any agreement.[10] The Canadians had already taken unilateral steps to protect the home market by placing an embargo on Soviet imports in February 1931, prompting immediate retaliation form Moscow.[11]

The British were unsure how to respond. The Cabinet was divided. The National Liberals and National Labour disliked trade restrictions. The Conservatives were largely in favour. Initially, Chancellor of the Exchequer Neville Chamberlain opposed Bennett.[12] But the latter was well aware that the British were loath to fail at Ottawa and Chamberlain was obliged to give way and agree to denunciation of the temporary Anglo-Soviet trade agreement finalised in 1930, in return for acceptance by Canada of imperial preferences.[13] The Cabinet swallowed this with difficulty. The decision was not confirmed until the 12 October.[14] Five days later Bogomolov received the bad news, which came as a considerable shock to both him[15] and Litvinov, who described it as a great blow,[16] for the embassy's recent discussions with Simon had indicated the unlikelihood of such a measure.[17] Yet the blow was softened by the fact that the note abrogating the agreement referred to Britain's anxiety to further trade between the two countries and its willingness to "enter into discussions upon the situation created by the denunciation",[18] so the Russians could be fairly certain that worse was not to follow and that this was merely a manoeuvre prior to negotiations.[19] Thus the *Pravda* editorial on the 21 October, entitled "The Diehards are Destroying the Basis of Anglo-Soviet Trade", focused less on the Diehards than on the "MacDonald-Thomas group", whom it accused of "acting time and time again in the role of the most infamous lackey of the sworn enemies of the English working-class". This was a sign that the polemics had been relegated to minions in the Comintern as a convenient device for assaulting Social Democracy, leaving others free for more pressing business. For, however much the Conservatives disliked dealing with Moscow, they really had no choice; they were prisoners of Britain's new-found penury. The Depression had taken its toll of British prosperity whilst, for all its defects, the five-year plan had secured the Russians considerable advantage in dealing with a divided West, provided, of course, the West remained divided.

Another side to Moscow's success in dealing with Britain was the striking growth in its prestige amongst the intelligentsia, a phenomenon which was to reach its apogee in the mid to late thirties, reinforced by Soviet leadership of the anti-Fascist camp. Ironically it was amongst Labour Party intellectuals, otherwise derided by the Comintern, that Soviet influence began to spread. As Beatrice Webb noted in December 1931: "it will be an ironic development if the highly respectable Fabian Society — the Upper Chamber of the Labour and Socialist Movement — becomes the protagonist of Soviet Communism in Great Britain and its guarantor in the Second International".[20] By March of the following year she recorded: "what little intellect there is, be it noted, is in the Fabian Society and is swinging towards Soviet Communism – to the horrors of continental Socialists".[21]

This was a new development. At the outset the same Fabians had greeted the Bolshevik revolution with mixed feelings, for it spelt the destruction of not only bourgeois but also Social Democracy in Russia. Realising after Bolshevik victory in the civil war that the regime was here to stay, a rapprochement was attempted. But the gap between the two sides turned out to be an abyss. With the prominent exception of George Bernard Shaw, who typically claimed to have been a Bolshevik before they had been invented, and who admired Mussolini's Fascism as much as Russian Bolshevism, the early twenties found the Fabians out of sympathy with Lenin's Russia. It had nothing positive to offer. Furthermore, as Beatrice Webb wrote: "the theory and practice of the Russian Soviet Government is wholly inconsistent with the theory and practice of British Socialism. We British Socialists believe in political industrial democracy: we do not believe in revolution through the dictatorship of a minority".[22] The turning-point was the implementation of the first five-year plan in 1929. Combined with the shock of the Great Crash in the West that autumn, it completely revolutionised attitudes towards the Soviet Union amongst the Fabians. What struck them was that whereas in Russia one saw the more equitable distribution of underproduction, in the capitalist world one found the less equitable distribution of overproduction.[23] There was also a glaring contrast between the spirit of resignation prevalent amongst the British elite and the buoyant optimism apparently displayed by the rulers and their followers in Russia. Although certain qualms remained,[24] The Webbs eventually resolved the dilemma by publicly ignoring the bad and exaggerating the good. Others, like Kingsley Martin, editor of *The New Statesman*, came to do the same. As Keynes drily noted: "When a doubt rises, it is swallowed down if possible. . . . This is the right spirit in which to visit Russia, if one wants to enjoy oneself".[25]

This good will stemmed from the conviction that to a large extent the Russians were in effect practising a Fabian conception of socialism, without, that is, the "inevitability of gradualness", at a time when even Beatrice Webb confessed doubts as to "even the practicability of gradualness".[26] The Webbs had always sought a managed form of socialism — not the guild socialism of G.D.H. Cole, but the socialism in their *Constitution of a Socialist Commonwealth*. The apparent similarity in purpose between their own ideals and the Stalinist structure led them to condone the ruthlessness rejected so decisively a few years before, the implication being that Britain would be better off with a dose of it as well.

Doubts within the West about the West left a vacuum ingeniously filled by the Soviet authorities, who embarked on a massive publicity campaign to sell the new Russia to the West. It became the fashion to visit the USSR by courtesy of Intourist, and many had already made the trip by May 1932 when the Webbs departed for the country. The Russians had made considerable propaganda out of the visit by George Bernard Shaw from July to August 1931. An *Izvestiya* cartoonist wryly noted that the English bourgeoisie were as a result extremely "shawked" (*Angliiskaya burzhuaziya chrezvychaino Shoukirovana*).[27] The Fabians saw what they hoped to see in Russia. Unable to realise the ideal at home, they soon satisfied themselves with idealising the real abroad.

That the Soviet authorities took this phenomenon extremely seriously is evident from Litvinov's conversation with Maisky, on the eve of his departure for Britain to take up his post as polpred. The tenor of the general instructions he received was to extend the Soviet embassy's contacts across as broad a range as possible, including not only "the narrow circle of persons connected with the Foreign Office but also a number of members of the Government, prominent politicians, people of the City and representatives of the cultural world".[28] Maisky himself had been chosen as an Anglophile. As the British envoy in Helsinki – Maisky's previous posting — noted: "he has the most friendly feelings towards Great Britain ... because of his good reception when he was a political refugee in 1912 and again during the war". Maisky told him that "his Government are aware of his feelings and that his appointment must be regarded as evidence of their intention to cultivate the best possible relations with His Majesty's Government".[29] This is also what Litvinov told the British ambassador in Moscow.[30] Maisky received his instructions from Litvinov sometime during the first half of October; news of Britain's abrogation of the trade agreement had not yet reached Moscow. The Soviet response to the news was far more phlegmatic than during similar occasions in the past. The reason for this was only partly due to the evident willingness of the British to negotiate. It was also attributable to the fact that the international situation as a whole was seemingly making steady progress.

11 False Optimism on the Eve of Hitler's Victory

The anxieties of early summer had given way to an autumn of illusions. But this became apparent only with the traumatic reawakening caused by Hitler's unexpected ascent to power at the end of January 1933. For two inversely related sets of events conspired to delude the Soviet leadership — distracted by a crisis within the Party over the famine and eager for good omens from any quarter[1] — into the belief that "the balance of forces in the international arena" had "altered" to their "advantage".[2] Firstly, the threat of German revanchism sufficed to cajole both Poland and France into a final settlement of their differences with the USSR; and, secondly, those who had always held strong reservations about the unalloyed utility of extreme nationalist sentiment in Germany, because of its close association with fierce anti-Bolshevism, had their fears assuaged by the abrupt decline in Nazi electoral appeal.

Germany in the autumn of 1932 saw the National Socialist Party increasingly rent by dissent over the leadership's determination to pursue a parliamentary rather than insurrectionist route to power. The resultant discontent, expressed in defections and expulsions from the party, played into the hands of those who never acknowledged the real dangers represented by the NSDAP. At the Comintern executive's XII plenum in August doubts were raised about the wisdom of existing policies. The critics, such as Humbert-Droz of the Swiss Communist Party, were roundly condemned by Knorin, head of the Comintern's Central European secretariat, for "mistakenly" thinking "that the fundamental process which is occurring now in Germany is the growth of Fascism". It was, he said, "laughable to see only Hitler on the street".[3] Other commentators, and not only in the Soviet capital,[4] speculated on "The Beginning of the Decomposition of Hitler's Party".[5] Hopes thus rose in Moscow that Nazi losses might translate into gains for the KPD. The dramatic fall in votes for the National Socialists at the Reichstag elections on the 6 November from 13 700 000 to 11 700 000 – giving them 196 as against the previous 230 seats – then confirmed this misplaced sense of optimism; for it was accompanied by a significant increase in support for the Communists, who received six million as against 5 300 000 votes gained the previous July – giving them an additional eleven seats, a total of 100. This was widely heralded as the beginning of the end for Hitler. In France, for example, Léon Blum, leader of the Socialists, declared that Hitler was not only "excluded from power" but excluded even "from hope of power", whilst on the extreme Right *l'Action Française* spoke of "the twilight of Hitler".[6] Not surprisingly *Pravda*, too, joined the chorus and rashly pointed to the coming "sunset of the 'National Socialist Party'",[7] and all the signs are that no one in Moscow was taking seriously the warnings reaching them from Khinchuk, the recalcitrant Cassandra in Berlin. His revelation that Schleicher was plotting to ensure not only Nazi entry into the government, but also that "Hitler himself heads the Cabinet",[8] apparently failed to stir the Kremlin from its indifference. After all, had not ambassador Dirksen assured them that President Hindenburg would never let Hitler attain power?[9]

The ratification of the Polish–Soviet non-aggression pact on the 26–7 November and the signature of the Franco-Soviet non-aggression pact on the 29th[10] further boosted Soviet self-confidence. Hailed as "A New Victory for the USSR's Peace Policy", Poland's move was prematurely welcomed as "a direct consequence of the massive growth in the economic and political power of the USSR"; this was a fervent wish rather than a matter of fact. More to the point, *Pravda* also argued that:

> The conclusion of the treaty ... reflects those shifts and regroupings within the camp of imperialism which result from the worsening of contradictions between states in the capitalist world, particularly the increasingly evident *bankruptcy of the Versailles system*. ... In this connexion, it is worth noting the acute exacerbation of Polish-German contradictions.[11]

Increasingly disturbed by events in Germany, the Poles had gone ahead with ratification despite the failure of Bucharest and Moscow to come to terms. Soviet–Romanian negotiations still stumbled at the Bessarabian hurdle, and the elevation of the mercurial Titulescu to the post of Foreign Minister brought all progress to a halt. Evidently to relieve constant pressure on themselves to settle with Moscow, the Romanians advised Warsaw to press on with ratification, secure in the knowledge that the Polish-Soviet pact would in no way supersede the Polish–Romanian treaty of alliance. The French, too, had hitherto waited on Bucharest, impatiently pacing the corridors, vainly hoping to maintain the cohesion of their alliance system in the face of the growing threat from Germany and the blandishments of Litvinov.[12]

There was therefore a large amount of truth in Moscow's claim that "*in fact if someone had to change their orientation, it was not us.*",[13] and the Russians continued to assert their opposition to the Versailles system *in principle*; but the fact remained that this rapprochement with the Versailles Powers was a first step towards a fundamental realignment of Soviet foreign policy. This was certainly how it was seen in Berlin, and in Moscow it aroused strong misgivings amongst the Germanophile element. For whilst there had always been those, even among the military,[14] who favoured a reorientation in this direction, the Rapallo tradition still weighed heavily in both Party and state. A despatch from the French ambassador, Dejean, dated the 19 December 1932, throws some light on this question. "Mr Litvinov", he wrote, "has succeeded in imposing his policy, and this policy is based on a reciprocity of interests between the USSR and France. According to information which the embassy has obtained, this fait accompli has not put an immediate end to dissensions within the Comintern, certain of whose members, with no part in the real responsibilities of power, and with a different appreciation of the international situation from Mr Litvinov, remain, through a kind of momentum of their own, the advocates of *an exclusively German orientation.*"[15]

It would, however, be false to assume that the sophisticates of the Narkomindel saw the situation purely in terms of either, or; for even those wedded and glued to the Rapallo policy nonetheless recognised the value of better relations with the Versailles Powers as useful pressure on Berlin, reminding the Germans that they could not afford to neglect their erstwhile companions. Indeed, as Krestinsky – a firm advocate of Rapallo – pointed out in a letter to Khinchuk at the beginning of December: "I am convinced that, now the Franco-Soviet pact has been signed, the German Government will begin to think seriously about the need to speed up its ratification of last year's Moscow protocol."[16] He then pursued the matter further in conversation with Dirksen two days later.[17] And whilst Germanophiles at the Narkomindel were not averse to accepting a tactical realignment as a means of exerting pressure on Berlin, Litvinov was also sufficiently a realist to value extreme nationalism in Germany, though amongst the military rather than the Nazis, as a barrier to German integration with the West. Italy's ambassador to Moscow, Attolico, recorded the following conversation with Litvinov on the 23 August:

> I ... passed on to talk of the possibility of a change in the situation should Hitler come to power, adding immediately, in the form of a premiss, my conviction that "even if Hitler comes to power, the fundamental lines of German policy vis-à-vis the USSR would not change". Litvinov did not offer any opposition to this hint of mine. He confined himself to saying: "I don't know". "However", he added, "I have no more faith in Hitler than in von Papen. Perhaps, from the foreign policy point of view, an improvement, i.e. the adoption of a clearer position on all the great international questions, could be expected more readily with a military dictatorship under von Schleicher or whoever replaces him at the head of the Reichswehr".[18]

Schleicher's appointment as Chancellor on the 2 December therefore came as welcome news to both currents of opinion within Moscow. Symptomatic of this was the loud silence in the Soviet press with regard to the likely direction of his foreign policy, in stark contrast to speculation on his probable domestic policies and also to former practice in relation to previous changes of government. The dire warning in *Pravda* that Schleicher's would prove "a Government which would increase its terrorisation of the Communist Party"[19] undoubtedly reflected anxieties within the Comintern, but it bore little relationship to the concerns of the Narkomindel. On the 19 December Litvinov made clear to Foreign Minister Neurath that his Government dissociated Schleicher's domestic repression from its overriding interest in maintaining the Rapallo relationship.[20]

These circumstances undoubtedly encouraged the Russians to believe that they could now concentrate their efforts on the consolidation of their position in the Far East to assure themselves of the breathing-space necessary to recover from famine and the economic dislocation consequent upon excessively rapid and unbalanced rates of growth. Progress here was still hampered by Soviet military weakness relative to the Japanese and absence of US diplomatic recognition,[21] compounded by the unavailability of a willing ally in the region. Instead the Soviet Government had to content itself with a lesser victory — the re-establishment of diplomatic relations with Nanking on the 12 December, acclaimed as a further step forwards in the USSR's peace policy.[22] Its value was underlined by the bitter reaction it elicited from the Japanese, who resented even so cautious a reassertion of the Russian presence in China. For the announcement of the pact gave rise to an acrimonious exchange between Litvinov and Matsuoka, Japan's representative at the League. Congratulating him on his success, Matsuoka then sarcastically suggested that for this the Russians had only the Japanese to thank, for they had "so scared China" that Nanking had been forced to turn to the Soviet Union. Japan, he continued indelicately, was now attempting to bring about a rapprochement between Moscow and Washington. Somewhat startled at such audacity Litvinov, never at a loss for words on such occasions, politely but icily enquired whether Japan also intended to "scare America" and whether Matsuoka's outbursts at the League were framed with this in mind.[23] Meanwhile in Tokyo the head of the Foreign Ministry's press department accused the Russians of attempting to intimidate Japan and warned Nanking that "today more than ever China should be keeping itself at a distance from the Soviet Union".[24] The Soviet Government was now informed that the time was "not yet ripe" for negotiations on a Russo-Japanese non-aggression pact.[25] This came as an alarming reminder to Moscow that its position in the Far East was still far from secure. Not until the USSR had healed the breach with the USA and built up its economic and military power in Asia could the Russians feel confident on that score, provided there was no simultaneous threat from the West. But by then, of course, the illusory stability in Europe had been shattered by Hitler's ascent to power and the Soviet Government faced the frightening prospect of a war on two fronts.

12 Conclusion

How did the balance stand at home and abroad at the end of 1932? To what extent were the Russians materially and psychologically ready to meet the challenge posed so dramatically by Hitler's unexpected accession to power at the beginning of 1933?

The traumatic experiences of 1930 and then the reawakening of war fears from 1931 to 1932 only underlined the Soviet Union's isolation in a hostile environment. No revolution emerged to rescue Russia from its overwhelming and alarming vulnerability to the outside world. In fact the Bolsheviks were frightened rather than relieved to hear of insurrectionist talk in Western Europe. Instead of asking what would happen should a revolutionary attempt succeed, they appear to have morosely contemplated the fearful consequences of failure – a revival of military intervention from the West. As a consequence revolutionary internationalism lived on only in name. It was all but dead, though a funeral had yet to be arranged. The contrast with what was happening within Russia is striking. There the people were being driven relentlessly and ruthlessly along the hard road to industrialisation – a revolution from above – in a climate of growing radicalism, albeit of a sectarian variety and under autocratic rule. Yet foreign policy was increasingly cautious and conservative, dictated by the overriding need for peace until the great experiment at home was complete. In these conditions the Russians could not even afford the luxury of isolationism – much as it matched the xenophobic attitudes of those who had spent their pre-revolutionary years underground in Russia rather than abroad in exile. This was indubitably Stalin's outlook, yet Litvinov was largely free to pursue an outgoing foreign policy. He matched his master in his cynical contempt for the prospects for world revolution and therefore shared his belief in the need for "socialism in one country", but instead of leading a retreat into fortress Russia, Litvinov pressed hard for greater contacts with the West, confident in the pursuit of common interest with the capitalist camp rather than fearful of the potential menace it represented. Peaceful co-existence reappeared in the Soviet diplomatic vocabulary to become to watchword abroad of Russia under reconstruction, and before long this obsession with the need for peace would shift the USSR from its long-standing role as a vociferous opponent of the territorial status quo in Europe to that of its most vigilant guardian. Everything was subordinate to industrialisation.

But what had so far been achieved? It was the country's misfortune that by 1933 this agonising process was not as advanced as Stalin had originally anticipated. Although, for the purpose of boosting morale, the five-year plan was misleadingly declared complete at the end of 1932, the truth was more prosaic. Many of the more ambitious projects, in particular, were still under construction. Two years of bad harvests – in 1931 and 1932 – further exacerbated the disastrous impact of forced collectivisation on the state of the countryside. The result was a ruinous famine. There were problems elsewhere as well. Falling receipts from the exportation of raw materials into a declining world market left the country with less foreign currency than expected, at a time when payments were due on extensive foreign credits advanced to finance capital goods imported to fuel industrialisation. This confronted the Russians with the alarming prospect of defaulting and thereby wrecking their hitherto impeccable reputation in international money markets. There can be no doubt that these economic problems gnawed at the sinews of the USSR's international position.

However, it would be wrong to adopt too pessimistic a view. Much had already been achieved during these years, a fact readily acknowledged by informed foreign observers. The Italian ambassador, for example, referred to 1931 as "the year in which Europe has finally conceded that Soviet Russia was no longer a passing political phenomenon ... whereas until 1930 the entire world swore by the failure of the 'piatiletka' [five year plan], in 1931 everyone ended up believing exactly the opposite".[1] This impression was only partly eroded by the economic crisis of 1932, as is indicated by this comment from the level-headed Commercial Counsellor at the British embassy: "things may be bad, but they are not ... 100 per cent bad. In spite of all the mess that undoubtedly exists ... something tangible is being accomplished".[2]

None the less the adverse conditions of 1932 did mean that it was still dangerously premature for the Soviets to claim that their progress in the international arena was attributable directly to their economic progress at home. An editorial in *Pravda* on the 25 December 1932 entitled "A Five-Year Plan for Enhancing the International Position of Soviet Power" made this claim. Yet it would take more than one good harvest to rectify the frightening effects of the famine and at least a further two years for the USSR to reap the international benefits of industrialisation, in terms of an enormously enhanced defence potential, world-wide prestige and the bases of a near-autarchic economy that would withstand the ravages of war. In the meantime, however, the Great Depression had propelled the world into international complications of bewildering complexity, at a time when the Soviet leadership was too engrossed in the resolution of domestic difficulties to respond rapidly enough to the problems they faced abroad. Worst of all, perhaps, the year 1932 closed with the illusion widespread in Moscow that, with the exception of the Far East, the international situation was moving to their advantage – a view shattered very shortly by the speed with which Germany headed for Armageddon, dragging the rest of Europe in its wake.

Appendix 1: The State of the Red Army and the Retreat from Forced Collectivisation of Agriculture

The rumour current in Moscow was that Voroshilov had demanded an end to forced collectivisation because of its harmful effects on the armed forces. There are several sources testifying to this, including the memoirs of a Yugoslav Communist in Russia at the time[1] as well as reports reaching the Foreign Office in London.[2] However, these rumours do not appear to have been entirely accurate, as we will see below. Nevertheless there is no disputing the fact of widespread unrest within the Red Army. A despatch from Ovey, the British ambassador to Moscow, dated the 28 March 1930 tells us that:

> certain members of the Government, whose power has made itself felt in the recent changes in the direction of a more reasonable policy towards the farmers, the devout, and the 'lichentsi' have for some time known of the latent disaffection in the army. Aware of this fact, and convinced that the Polish Government were equally well informed on the matter, they naturally felt that the opportunity would be too good a one for the military party in Poland to miss in their plan to promote a quarrel.[3]

The French were equally convinced of this, and a report from the Sûreté Générale repeated the Voroshilov rumour, adding that "at the present time the Soviet authorities are no longer able to hide that the state of morale of the red soldiers is very bad. ... Even the Communist elements in the army have succumbed to anti-governmental tendencies".[4] Italian diplomats, possessed of far better contacts with the regime, received a more detailed account of the whole affair, which denies any direct initiative by Voroshilov. According to this, a session of the Central Committee – more probably an expanded meeting of the Politburo – took place at the end of February:

> Gamarnik, head of political education in the Red Army, delivered a powerful speech declaring that the situation created as a consequence of the policy of "liquidating the kulaks" and of agricultural collectivisation to the bitter end, demanded by Stalin, had given rise to an incurable discontent amongst the soldiers – in large part the sons of peasants – who did not conceal their resentment of the Soviet Government. Thus either the system changed or they would no longer be able to count on the Red Army.

The report added that he was supported in this demand by Bubnov, his predecessor, now Commissar of Education for the RSFSR. Stalin was silent. Immediately after the session he called on the Politburo to pronounce on the criticisms made of him and only Molotov spoke in his defence. A vote was taken and seven members voted against the policy hitherto pursued, leaving only two in favour (Stalin and Molotov). Apparently Stalin then asked for 24 hours in which to reach a decision, and during that time he wrote the article "Dizziness from Success", which called a halt to forced collectivisation, published in *Pravda* on the 2 March, without consulting his colleagues. The Italian ambassador, in his communication to Rome, stated that his source for this information was an "authoritative" one,[5] and it was later confirmed by another Soviet source.[6]

Appendix 2: The Search for US Recognition

The Soviet decision to curtail trade with the USA as a means of exerting pressure on Washington to grant diplomatic recognition was made in the autumn of 1931.[1] As a result, US exports to the USSR dropped dramatically from their level of over 180 million roubles in 1931 to only 24.8 million in 1932.[2] This move was well calculated, for the opposition Democrats soon used the issue as a stick with which to beat the Hoover administration. As early as the 4 January 1932 Representative Rainey, Democrat leader in the House, had already warned that:

> If we have Communist demonstrations this winter in our large cities the main cause will be closed factories. The way to fight communism in this country is to reopen the factories. The only way to do this is to get markets abroad; and Russia is the largest and the best one.[3]

And as Soviet reprisals began to make their impact, the demand for recognition of the USSR grew more compelling. On the 21 April Democrat floor leader, Senator Robinson (Arkansas), called for recognition "as one feature in the policy of promoting amicable international relations and stimulating our foreign commerce".[4] It was thus to be expected that when Roosevelt won the Presidential elections some progress in this direction would soon be made. But the Democrats were too preoccupied with more pressing domestic matters to pay urgent and close attention to Russian demands. When the Soviet Union's unofficial emissary, Skvirsky, met with Colonel House (now at Roosevelt's side) early in December 1932, he was brushed off with the promise that the new administration would consider the issue of relations with the USSR immediately after the inauguration, in March 1933.[5] Not until a further meeting with House (along with Welles) on the 10 January 1933 was Skvirsky fairly certain that Roosevelt would grant recognition.[6]

Notes and References

CHAPTER 1   THE BASES OF FOREIGN POLICY
           UNDER STALIN

1. "The Tasks of Business Executives", speech delivered 4.2.31: J.V.Stalin, *Works*, vol. 13 (Moscow, 1955) pp. 40–1.
2. Yu. Klyuchnikov, "Problema garantii", *Mezhdunarodnaya Letopis'*, no. 10–11 (1925) pp. 34–65.
3. Strang (Moscow) to Henderson (London), 30.8.30: *Documents on British Foreign Policy 1919–1939*, 2nd Series, vol. VII, edited by E.L.Woodward and Rohan Butler (London, 1958) doc. 96.
4. See pp. 25–6; also Appendix 1.
5. *Izvestiya*, 26.7.30.
6. E. Varga, "Novyi agrarnyi krizis", *Mirovoe Khozyaistvo i Mirovaya Politika*, no. 8–9 (1929) pp. 13–22.
7. B.R., "Ekonomicheskie vzaimootnosheniya SSSR s kapitalisticheskimi stranami za 15 let", ibid., no. 10 (1932) pp. 46–71.
8. See p. 44.
9. *Dokumenty Vneshnei Politiki SSSR*, vol. XIV, edited by P.I.Yershov *et al.* (Moscow, 1968) doc. 163.
10. From an interview with the *New York Times* correspondent in Moscow at the end of November 1929: Walter Duranty, *STALIN AND CO: The Politburo – The Men Who Run Russia* (London, 1949) p.51.
11. See p. 55.
12. See p. 108.
13. Ovey (Moscow) to Henderson (London), 3.6.30: *DBFP*, op. cit., doc. 88.
14. From a resolution passed at the XVI congress of the Soviet Communist Party, 2.7.30: *DVP SSSR*, vol. XIII, edited by G.K. Deev et al. (Moscow, 1967) doc. 237.
15. E.H.Carr, *Foundations of a Planned Economy 1926–1929*, vol. 3, part I (London, 1976) chs 70 and 71.
16. Editorial, "Na vysshuyu stupen' (k itogam rasshirennogo prezidiuma IKKI)", *Kommunisticheskii Internatsional*, no. 7 (10.3.30) pp. 3–8.
17. See p. 57.
18. The anxiety with which the Soviets watched the Balkan states meet to confer in Athens from the 5 to the 12 October 1930 over the establishment of a Balkan federation testifies to the reality of such fears. For an account of this episode, based on material from the Soviet archives, see N. Zhukovsky, *Na Diplomaticheskom Postu* (Moscow, 1973) pp. 123–8.
19. See ch. 6.

CHAPTER 2   THE CONDUCT OF SOVIET DIPLOMACY

1. I.M.Maisky, *Lyudyi, Sobytiya, Fakty* (Moscow, 1973) p. 129.
2. "Shestidesyatiletie M.M.Litvinova", *Izvestiya*, 17.7.36.
3. "Vydayushchiisya sovetskii diplomat", *Pravda*, 5.12.62.
4. "Shestidesyatiletie M.M.Litvinova", *Izvestiya*, 17.7.36.
5. An amusing fictionalised account of how they met and fell in love is given by Ivy in the form of a short story, "Call it Love", contained in *She Knew She Was Right* (London, 1971) pp. 60–92.
6. R.H.Ullman, *Anglo-Soviet Relations 1917–1921*, vol. 1: *Intervention and the War* (London, 1961) pp. 60 and 79–81.
7. Soviet diplomats were also impressed with his "iron logic": Surits, "Uchenik Stalina", *Izvestiya*, 17.7.36.
8. Grandi's account of his meeting with Litvinov in November 1930: *I Documenti Diplomatici Italiani, 7 Serie: 1922–1935*, vol. IX, edited by Ruggero Moscati *et al.* (Rome, 1975) doc. 411.
9. See, for example, Ovey (Moscow) to Henderson (London), 10.3.30: *DBFP*, op. cit., doc. 73.
10. Radek, "Velikii diplomat proletariata", *Izvestiya*, 17.7.36.
11. V.I.Lenin, *Collected Works*, vol. 45 (Moscow, 1970) 720n.
12. Louis Fischer, *Men and Politics: An Autobiography* (New York, 1941) p. 127.
13. Maisky, op. cit., p. 138.
14. Kollontai, "Diplomat-stakhanovets", *Izvestiya*, 17.7.36.
15. Maisky, op. cit., p. 138.
16. See, for example, the account of Chicherin's interview with Potemkin, following the latter's appointment as polpred to Athens, given in N. Zhukovsky, op. cit., pp. 102–6.
17. This information "from a reliable source" found its way into the Italian embassy in Moscow – Cerruti (Moscow) to Rome, 18.1.30: Ministèro degli Affari Esteri, *Archivio Storico Diplomatico: Affari Politici 1919–1930*, Russia (1930), pacco 1558; also note 30.
18. Victor Serge, "Litvinov", *Esprit*, 1.6.39.
19. Krestinsky, "Boets", *Izvestiya*, 17.7.36.
20. See note 17.
21. The British ambassador's despatch, sent after receiving news of Litvinov's appointment, contains the following passage:

> An interesting rumour has just reached me from a well-informed source that the appointment of M. Litvinov was, up to the last moment, extremely doubtful. There was a strong movement in important circles in the Kremlin to make a clean sweep of the Presidium [*sic*] of the Commissariat for Foreign Affairs, with the exception of M. Karakhan. The Commissar was to be Kirov, an extremist, who is a member of the Politburo and of the Central Committee of the Communist party, and who held high military commands during the civil war. The other members of the Collegium were to have been individuals of the same type. The Narkomindel was fully aware of the danger overhanging them, but at the eleventh hour other counsels prevailed, and the 'safe' M.

Litvinov was appointed with an entourage of moderates.
– Ovey (Moscow) to Henderson (London), 28.7.30: *DBFP*, op. cit., doc. 92.

22. I am grateful to Mr Arfon Rees of Keele University for information (as yet unpublished) on this point.

23. Lenin referred to the Narkomindel as "the best of our commissariats", firstly, "because diplomats of the old stamp could not remain there to any noticeable degree; secondly, because we selected people there anew, selected them by entirely new standards, by their fitness for the new tasks; thirdly, because there, in the Foreign Commissariat, we do not have, as in other commissariats, that plethora of haphazardly selected employees who, practically speaking, have inherited all the old qualities of officialdom; and fourthly, because the Foreign Commissariat is working under the guidance of our Central Committee. This, as a matter of fact, is the only one of our commissariats that has been fully renovated and that is really working for the workers' and peasants' government and in the spirit of that government, and not merely giving the impression of working for it, while actually, in the main, working against it or in the wrong spirit" – "What Should We Do With the W.P.I.?", 13.1.23: V.I.Lenin, *Collected Works*, vol. 42 (Moscow, 1969) pp. 437–8.

24. In April 1930 Rotshtein lost his post as head of the Narkomindel's press department and in July also lost his place in the collegium: *FO* 371/14887.

25. Radek, *Izvestiya*, 17.7.36.

26. Krestinsky, ibid.

27. Surits, ibid.

28. Lapinsky, "Neutomimy borets za mir", ibid.

29. Krestinsky, ibid.

30. As late as the 2 July the Italian ambassador reported to Rome that he had it on good authority that it was still improbable Litvinov would succeed Chicherin. The name of Rykov was once again being canvassed – Cerruti (Moscow) to Rome, 2.7.30: *ASD*, loc. cit. A further report from the Italian embassy is worth quoting. On the 24 July Persico, Cerruti's deputy, wrote that:

> Most of the pressure came from the Soviet ambassador in Berlin, Krestinsky, who sought the position of Commissar. Faced with this possibility Litvinov declared that he wanted to retire and requested a long holiday which was not granted him. The same source has assured me that right up until mid-day on the 21 instant, Litvinov had no knowledge of the decisions of the Politburo of the party and the central executive committee.

However, it should be noted that Persico does not testify as to the reliability of his informant – Persico (Moscow) to Rome, 24.7.30: ibid.

31. Because of his past association with Trotsky and his execution during the great terror in 1937, Krestinsky's name was excised from Soviet history until Maisky reviewed his life and achievements in *Izvestiya*, 27.10.63. For further details of his career: *Bol'shaya Sovetskaya Entsiklopediya*, vol. 13, pp. 393–4.

32. There appears to be some dispute about Karakhan's actual date of birth. M.S.Kapitsa, the noted Soviet sinologist, gives it as the 2 February, whilst

the *Bol'shaya* (vol. 11) gives it as the 1 February. For Kapitsa's work, see below, note 33.

33. From Litvinov's letter to Chicherin, 31.10.25, cited in Kapitsa, "Lev Karakhan (1889–1937)", *Vidnye Sovetskie Kommunisty – Uchastniki Kitaiskoi Revolyutsii* (Moscow, 1970) pp. 5–21.

34. Cerruti, now ambassador in Berlin, obtained this information from Soviet sources (in confidence) – Cerruti (Berlin) to Rome, 20.12.32: *ASD*, URSS (1932), b.5, f.1.2.

35. *Izvestiya*, 12.5.33.

36. Payart (Moscow) to Paul-Boncour (Paris), 30.5.33: Ministère des Affaires Étrangères, *Archives Diplomatiques*, EUROPE 1930–40, URSS, 1012. This issue will be discussed in the following volume.

37. *1934. Annuaire Diplomatique du Commissariat du Peuple pour les Affaires Étrangères* (Moscow, 1935?).

38. Ovey (Moscow) to Henderson (London), 31.12.29: *DBFP*, op. cit., doc. 51.

39. Chicherin to Lenin (undated), cited by Kapitsa: as note 33.

40. A. Barmine, *Memoirs of a Soviet Diplomat* (London, 1938) p. 155.

41. This information has had to come from a variety of sources, none of them entirely satisfactory – Attolico (Moscow) to Rome, 14.3.34: *ASD*, URSS (1934), b.14, f.1.5; *Who Was Who in the USSR* edited by H.Schulz et al. (New Jersey, 1972); and *Diplomaticheskii Slovar'*, vol. III, edited by A.F.Miller *et al.* (Moscow, 1973).

42. Entry in the Foreign Office's potted biographies of Soviet personalities: *FO* 371/14887.

43. Attolico, loc. cit.

44. Information on the subject of Stalin's secretariat is not easy to find. A former party official, A.Avtorkhanov, has produced a list of the secretariat's members as they stood in 1929, amongst which the only names that stand out with respect to foreign policy are Varga and Umansky. Umansky moved to head the Narkomindel's press and information department in the early thirties. Varga was head of the Institute of World Economy and World Politics (Communist Academy) and sat on the Comintern Executive Committee. Neither appears to have had much influence over policy. Varga was jokingly referred to amongst his peers as *fabrika statistiki* (statistics factory) because it was said that he could manufacture statistics for any case Stalin cared to make. Certainly Stalin's speeches on foreign affairs bear his hall-mark; but then these speeches in themselves rarely took a firm position on crucial foreign policy issues, at least during the period of the first five-year plan. For a rather exaggerated account of the significance of the secretariat at this time: A. Avtorkhanov, *Proiskhozhdenie partokratii*, vol. 2, *TsK i Stalin* (Frankfurt/Main, 1973) pp. 413–15. For the anecdote about Varga and a discussion of his role: M.N.Roy, *MEN I MET* (Bombay, 1968). It would appear that the secretariat became more significant later in the thirties with respect to foreign policy; but this will be discussed in a further volume.

45. One such example is Stalin's telegram to Surits, polpred in Ankara, in November 1930, concerning approaches made to the Soviet mission by the Polish ambassador. At the time of its despatch, Litvinov was busy at Geneva – Stalin (Moscow) to Surits (Ankara), 21.11.30: *DVP SSSR*, vol. XIII, doc. 415. For an example of the Commissar communicating directly with Stalin,

in respect of a non-aggression pact with Romania (autumn of 1932) – Litvinov (Geneva) to Stalin (Moscow) 3.10.32: ibid., vol. xv, edited by P.I.Yershov *et al.* (Moscow, 1969) doc. 389.

46. For instance, Krestinsky's letter to the Politburo in September 1931, containing proposals for curtailing trade with the USA – Krestinsky to the Politburo, 18.9.31: ibid., vol. xiv, doc. 267.

47. An interesting example of Litvinov's manoeuvring was his attempt to secure the USSR a place on the European commission of the League of Nations late in 1930. Conscious of the fact that his superiors did not unanimously favour such a move, he tried to enlist Italian help in obtaining an invitation which would enable him to win over the sceptics in the leadership. As he told Grandi:

> I must confess to you that opinion is divided in Moscow. Some are for participation, some are against. I am in favour, because I am persuaded of the advantages of being where one can carry on useful activity against France. If the invitation comes on the same plane as those of the other European countries, perhaps my inclination will end up prevailing. However, I can not undertake a formal commitment.

for source, see note 8.

48. The issue of Litvinov and Hitler's accession to power will be discussed extensively in the following volume.

49. Krestinsky, *Izvestiya*, 17.7.36.

CHAPTER 3   1930: CRISES AT HOME AND ABROAD

1. This phrase appears in "Novaya volna antisovetskikh vystuplenii imperialistov", an editorial in *Pravda*, 29.1.30. For the most comprehensive history of the collectivisation process: R.W.Davies, *The Industrialisation of Soviet Russia I: The Socialist Offensive — The Collectivisation of Soviet Agriculture 1929–1930* (London, 1980).

2. Alec Nove, *An Economic History of the USSR* (Penguin, London, 1972) ch. 8; not until the last quarter of the economic year, from July to September 1930, did industrial production begin to decline – Davies, op. cit., p. 372.

3. "Novaya volna . . .', cited in note 1.

4. "Idut kolonial'nye rezervy", *Pravda*, 7.1.30.

5. *DBFP*, op. cit., doc. 24; and *DVP SSSR*, vol. xii, edited by I.I.Agayants et al. (Moscow, 1967) doc. 303.

6. *Torgovo-Promyshlennaya Gazeta*, 6.4.29.

7. Quoted from the mission's subsequent report in W.P. and Z.Coates, *A History of Anglo-Soviet Relations* (London, 1943) p. 332.

8. E.H.Carr, *Foundations of a Planned Economy 1926–1929*, vol. 3, iii (1978) pp. 895–910.

9. "Ne mir, a voina", *Izvestiya*, 18.1.30. A similar interpretation also appeared in *Pravda*, 27.1.30.

10. "Itogi Gaagi", *Izvestiya*, 19.1.30.

11. Sovremennik, "Mezhdunarodnoe obozrenie", ibid., 27.1.30. Not until the

26 January, three days after Estrada, Mexico's acting Foreign Minister, had informed the press, did the Mexican chargé d'affaires in Moscow tell Litvinov of the decision — Litvinov's record of the conversation, 26.1.30: *DVP SSSR*, vol. XIII, doc. 30.

12. At the time, the Soviet authorities denied all knowledge of his disappearance, and since then the only public admission of their complicity appeared quite by chance in a letter published in the Soviet military newspaper. Referring to a former OGPU officer, Sergei Vasil'evich Puzitskii, Colonel-General Shimanov wrote that "He...brilliantly carried out the operation to arrest Kutepov" — *Krasnaya Zvezda*, 22.9.65.

13. An impressionistic account of events, verging on fiction but which utilises documents from the French police archives (now closed to the public), certainly indicates that the Sûreté was almost as much in the dark as everyone else: M. Grey, *Le general meurt à minuit: l'enlèvement de Koutiepov 1930 et de Miller 1937* (Paris, 1981). For the background to Kutepov's activities, including his use of terror to overthrow the Soviet regime, and OGPU's penetration of the organisation he controlled: S.L.Voitsekhovskii, *TREST: Vospominaniya i Dokumenty* (Canada, 1974), a useful work coloured by the author's personal involvement in the events he describes.

14. See, for example, *Le Matin* from the 29 January (the day Kutepov's disappearance was first reported in the paper) till late February 1930, including sensationalist "revelations" by Besedovsky, formerly a Soviet diplomat in Paris (ibid., 3.2.30). Litvinov was later to complain to the French ambassador in Moscow, Herbette, about the press campaign, saying that the French Government had "authorised" it — Herbette (Moscow) to Briand (Paris) 26.2.30: J. Herbette, *Ein französischer Diplomat über die bolschewistische Gefahr. Berichte des Botschafters der französischen Republik in Moskau in den Jahren 1927–1931* (Berlin, 1943) pp. 161–6.

15. Herbette (Moscow) to Briand (Paris) 14.10.30: Ministère des Affaires Etrangères, *AD*, 1054.

16. A senior member of the Soviet embassy at the time recalls that "if Kutyepov was spirited away by the GPU, as the evidence seemed to show, the thing was carried out in total independence of official Soviet representatives in Paris": A. Barmine, *One Who Survived* (New York, 1945) p. 186. The reaction of Soviet polpred Dovgalevsky to the Kutepovshchina in his cables to Moscow appears to bear this out. However, at least one of the embassy's diplomats, Arens (also an OGPU agent), seems to have been implicated – at least, according to Foreign Office sources: *FO* 371/14887. Arens was before long recalled to Moscow, and replaced Rotshtein as head of the Narkomindel's press and information department; it included within its sphere not merely press and information, but also the supervision of foreign journalists and the censorship of their despatches.

17. Dovgalevsky (Paris) to Moscow, 31.1.30: *DVP SSSR*, op. cit., doc. 38.

18. "Gde pravitel'stvo g. Tard'e?", *Izvestiya*, 3.2.30.

19. "Prigovor klassovoi nenavisti", ibid., 9.2.30.

20. Ovey (Moscow) to Henderson (London), 8.2.30: *DBFP*, op. cit., doc. 64.

21. Ovey (Moscow) to Henderson (London), 28.3.30: ibid., doc. 77.

22. Cerruti (Moscow) to Rome, 15.2.30: *ASD*, Russia (1930), loc. cit.

23. "Mezhdusobiya imperialistov i podgotovka voiny protiv SSSR", *Kommunisticheskii Internatsional*, No. 4 (10.2.30) pp. 3–11.
24. *Pravda*, 23.2.30.
25. As *Pravda* noted:

> The Red Army is, together with the working-class, taking an active part in socialist construction. It is training the socialist organisers of agriculture and participating in the preparation of cadres for socialist industry. . . . But its basic attention must be focused on military training.

   – "Na-strazhe sovetskikh rubezhei", ibid. The military journal *Voennyi Vestnik* also pointed to the Red Army's role in fighting the kulak, only to stress that "at the same time we must not forget our international position" and the Red Army's role "as one of the most important guarantees of peaceful socialist construction in the Soviet Union", particularly at a time when the war danger was "growing month by month" – an unsigned article entitled "Mezhdunarodnoe polozhenie i krasnaya armiya", *Voennyi Vestnik*, no. 5, 15.2.30.
26. Editorial, "Eshche o novom povorote politiki partii", ibid., no. 6, 25.2.30.
27. Herbette (Moscow) to Paris, 19.1.30: *AD*, 959.
28. This was uncovered by Britain's military attaché in Warsaw, Lt.Col. Martin, who, after the first reports of the scare from Bucharest, went there to discover their origins. There he saw, amongst others, the chief of the general staff, the chief of Intelligence, and the Polish military attaché. Mikhailowski admitted his role in creating the scare, and Colonel Florescu of Intelligence, when confronted with this, agreed that there was no danger of a Russian attack but "stated, however, that he could not put his military views on paper, as for political reasons it was necessary to magnify the RUSSIAN danger to obtain more money for the ROUMANIAN Army " – Erskine (Warsaw) to Henderson (London), 19.3.30: *FO* 371/14434. Italian sources confirm this. When the Polish ambassador to Moscow, Patek, returned from Warsaw on the 29 March, he told the Italian ambassador that Pilsudski had sent someone from the high command to inspect the Moldavian border. The man returned denying that any Russian forces were concentrated there – Cerruti (Moscow) to Rome, 30.1.30; Cerruti was also aware that the Poles had drawn the attention of both Prague and Bucharest to the dangers of a Soviet attack — Cerruti (Moscow) to Rome, 3.4.30: *ASD*, Russia (1930) pacco 1559.
29. Litvinov (Moscow) to Arosev (Prague), 28.2.30: *DVP SSSR*, op. cit. doc. 79.
30. Report from Duranty in Moscow, 3.3.30: *New York Times*, 4.3.30.
31. See Appendix 1.
32. E. Varga, "Gaagskaya konferentsiya i plan Yunga", *Mirovoe Khozyaistvo i Mirovaya Politika*, no. 10 (1929) pp. 10–32.
33. Quoted in "Gaaga No.2", editorial, *Pravda*, 3.1.30.
34. O.K. Flechtheim, *Die KPD in der Weimarer Republik* (Frankfurt am Main, 1969) p. 347.
35. At an expanded meeting of the presidium of the Comintern's executive committee held from the 8 to the 28 February 1930, the KPD was the only

party to be criticised by the Russians for "left" as well as "right" errors. No complete record of the proceedings has been published, but the substance of the decisions taken can be found in "Na vysshuyu stupen' (k itogam rashirennogo prezidiuma IKKI)", *Kommunisticheskii Internatsional*, no.7 (10.3.30) pp. 3–8. This was then followed by strong condemnation of *"sectarianism masked by left-wing phrases"* at a meeting of the KPD central committee in Berlin on the 20 March: *Pravda*, 25.3.30.

36. Severing, the Minister of the Interior, went so far as to claim that the KPD was "already bringing about its own disintegration": *AKTEN DER REICHSKANZLEI: Das Kabinett Müller 28. Juni 1928 bis 27. März 1930: Band 2: August 1929 bis März 1930*, edited by M. Vogt (Boppard am Rhein, 1970) doc. 452.

37. Litvinov (Moscow) to Brodovsky (Berlin), 7.2.30: *DVP SSSR*, op. cit., doc. 55.

38. H.L.Dyck, *Weimar Germany and Soviet Russia 1926–1933: A Study in Diplomatic Instability* (London, 1966) pp. 188–9.

39. Germanikus, "Germano-pol'skie soglasheniya", *Mezhdunarodnaya Zhizn'*, no. 5 (1930) pp. 26–41.

40. Report by Lt.Col. Martin, dated 16.4.30, and enclosed in Erskine (Warsaw) to Henderson (London), 20.4.30: *FO* 371/14824. The Italians received an identical impression of Polish attitudes – report by Col. Roatta, dated 24.3.30, enclosed in Martin-Franklin (Warsaw) to Rome, 3.4.30: *ASD*, 1558.

41. R. Dmowski, "SPRAWY ROSYJSKIE. I. Komiwojazer w klopocie", *Gazeta Warszawska*, 8.4.30; "II. Fantastyczne Pomysly", ibid., 9.4.30; "III. Nadzieje Niemieckie", ibid., 10.4.30; "IV. Rosja i Polska", ibid., 11.4.30; and "Rosja i Polska dokończenie", ibid., 12.4.30.

42. *Izvestiya*, 11.4.30.

43. Ver, "Dwa Fronty", *Gazeta Warszawska*, 11.4.30. This whole episode was watched with considerable interest from the British embassy in Warsaw: *FO* 371/14824.

44. Interview, 16.4.30: *New York Times*, 17.4.30.

45. Stomonyakov's record of the conversation, 13.6.30: *DVP SSSR*, op. cit., doc. 217.

46. *Cmd.* 3552, and *DVP SSSR*, op. cit., doc. 135.

47. Editorial, "Torgovoe soglashenie s Angliei", *Izvestiya*, 17.4.30.

48. Ovey (Moscow) to Henderson (London), 28.4.30: *DBFP*, op. cit., doc. 83; also Duranty's report in the *New York Times*, 18.4.30.

49. *Izvestiya*, 10.11.29; by January the British accepted that no progress would be made on this issue – Henderson (London), to Ovey (Moscow), 7.1.30: *DBFP*, op. cit., doc. 54.

50. The progress of the OGPU campaign can be followed in the documents of the Soviet border guards, who came under OGPU control: *Pogranichnye Voiska SSSR 1918–1928: Sbornik Dokumentov i Materialov*, edited by P.I.Zyryanov et al. (Moscow, 1973).

51. *Committee of Imperial Defence: Minutes of the 215 Meeting*, 22.7.26.

52. In 1921 the Russians arranged a subsidy to Amanullah of one million gold roubles (some £100 000 at 1921 prices) per annum: *FO* 371/14800.

53. A Foreign Office Northern Department memorandum discusses this episode: *FO* 371/14800.

54. *Pravda*, 23.2.30.

55. Vasil'evsky, "Fazy basmacheskogo dvizheniya v Srednei Azii", *Novyi Vostok*, no. 29 (1930) pp. 126–41.

56. From the report of the OGPU polpred in Central Asia on the activity of Ibrahim Beg and Ishan Khalif in Northern Afghanistan and their preparation of an attack on Bokhara, February 1930: *PV SSSR 1929–1938*, edited by P.I.Zyryanov et al. (Moscow, 1972) doc. 118. There is no evidence from the British side. These matters were not revealed to Foreign Office clerks, and both the FO and India Office archives have been so carefully weeded that any reference to such matters is impossible to trace. Steveni's reports from Meshed, which one can read, are restricted to those dealing with observations of Soviet troop movements in Central Asia and on the activities of various anti-Soviet elements, including the Basmachi. But as to British policy towards these groups: silence — which only tends to reinforce one's suspicions. For Steveni's reports, sent on a weekly basis, see notes 57–9 below.

57. Intelligence Summary, no.7, 15.3.30: *FO* 371/14540.

58. Ibid., no. 8 (22.3.30): ibid.

59. Ibid., no. 10 (5.4.30): ibid.

60. Maconachie (Kabul) to Henderson (London), 18.6.30: *FO* 371/14800. The aid took the form of 10 000 rifles and $200 000 in cash as a gift – exactly half of the Afghan request: ibid., and *CAB* 46 (30).

61. Dovgalevsky (Paris) to Moscow, 26.3.30: *DVP SSSR*, op. cit., doc. 115.

62. "Evènements du TONKIN et de l'ANNAM en 1930", Ministère des Colonies, Direction politique, 3° Bureau, no date: *Archives Nationales, Section Outre-mer: Indochine, Nouveau Fonds*, 323, 2628.

63. Herbette (Moscow) to Paris, 20.2.30: *AD*, 945.

64. Pasquier (Hanoi) to Paris (including both the Colonial and Foreign Ministries), 21.2.30: *AN*, 326, 2636.

65. Pasquier (Hanoi) to Paris, 23.2.30: ibid.

66. From his speech at the opening of the governing council in Indochina, reported in *Le Matin*, 2.1.30.

67. A.P.Shiltova and V.F.Mordvinov, *Natsional'no-Osvoboditel'noe Dvizhenie vo V'etname (1858–1945)* (Moscow, 1958) pp. 105–6.

68. Pasquier (Hanoi) to Paris, 27.2.30: *AN*, 322, 2611.

69. E.B.Kobelev, "Ho Chi-Minh – Velikii Syn V'etnama", *Novaya i Noveishaya Istoriya*, no. 5 (1976) pp. 84–100. Shiltova and Mordvinov (p. 106) do not give this date, merely stating that Ho Chi-Minh was in Hong Kong on the 6 January 1930 for this congress, as the Comintern's emissary. Ho had joined the PCF (French Communist Party) in 1920, represented the French colonies at the Krestintern (the short-lived Peasant International) congress in 1923, served on Borodin's staff in China the following year, and in 1925 founded a Communist grouping, the Vietnamese Association of Revolutionary Youth (Viet Nam Thanh Nien Cach Mang Dong Chi Hoi), but had worked essentially from China until the collapse of the Canton commune at the end of 1927 forced him to flee to Moscow.

70. See note 61.

71. In August Pasquier cabled Paris:

new agitators coming from Canton are arriving clandestinely in Indochina. The department knows from the latest monthly reports of the Sûreté's political branch that the Far Eastern section of the Third International has been in effective charge of the Indochinese Communist movement for four months.

- Pasquier (Saigon) to Paris, 23.8.30: *AN*, 326, 2636.
72. Pasquier (Hanoi) to Paris, 24.4.30: ibid.
73. Pasquier (Dalat) to Paris, 16.5.30: ibid.
74. *Journal Officiel de la République Française: Débats Parlementaires — Chambre de Députés*, 14.6.30, pp. 2496–508.
75. Between February and December 1930 there were 74 strikes and workers' demonstrations and, more importantly, 218 peasant uprisings between May and December: Shiltova and Mordvinov, op. cit., p. 107. See also "Les evènements depuis la révolte de Yen-Bey (1930 à 1933 inclus)", a note for the Minister by the Direction des affaires politiques, 4° Bureau: *AN*, 323, 2628.
76. See Hoang Quoc Viet, "Peuple Heroique", in *Récits de la resistance vietnamienne (1925–1945)* (Paris, 1966).

CHAPTER 4 THE USSR FACES A CAMPAIGN AGAINST DUMPING

1. In 1929 Germany occupied first place (22,7%); Britain, second place (14,3%), with the USA in third place (12,2%): *Vneshnyaya Torgovlya SSSR v Gody Dovoennykh Pyatiletok (1929–1940): Statisticheskii Sbornik* (Moscow, 1968).
2. Krestinsky to the Politburo, 18.9.31: *DVP SSSR*, vol. XIV, doc. 267.
3. Skvirsky (Washington) to Litvinov (Moscow), 2.5.30: ibid., vol. XIII, doc. 161.
4. *Izvestiya*, 31.7.30; reprinted in *DVP SSSR*, op. cit., doc. 278.
5. *Pravda*, 10.8.30.
6. Ibid.
7. H. Bulhak, "Polska A Rumunia 1918–1939", in *Przyjaźnie i Antagonizmy: Stosunki Polski z Państwami Sasiednimi w Latach 1918–1939*, edited by J. Zarnowski (Warsaw, 1977) p. 327.
8. *Pravda*, 28.8.30.
9. Dm. Bukhartsev, "Zelenaya blokada", ibid., 30.8.30.
10. Interview given to the press, enclosed in Preston (Kovno) to Knatchbull-Hugesson (Riga), 21.10.30: *FO* 371/14782.
11. "Memorandum sur l'Organisation d'un Régime d'Union fédérale européenne": *DBFP*, op. cit., doc. 186. For the origins of these ideas, see G. Suarez, *BRIAND: sa vie — son oeuvre*, VI, *1923–1932* (Paris, 1952) pp. 325–8.
12. Yurenev (Vienna) to Krestinsky (Moscow), 19.3.32: *DVP SSSR*, vol. XV, edited by P.I.Yershov et al. (Moscow, 1969) doc. 271.
13. Litvinov to missions in Austria, Britain, Germany, Greece, Denmark, Italy, Latvia, Lithuania, Norway, Finland, Sweden and Estonia, 7.6.30: ibid., vol. XIII, doc. 208.

14. Herbette (Moscow) to Paris, 26.7.30: *AD*, 945.
15. *Vneshnyaya Torgovlya*, op. cit. As with other countries there was, of course, no identity of method by which the Soviets and the French calculated the trade balance. Unlike the French (or for that matter the British), the Soviets included exports by companies operating beyond national frontiers, as well as colonial products, re-exports and invisibles: Note, 14.5.30: *AD*, 1054. The balance, nonetheless, still worked out to the relative advantage of the USSR, however the figures were calculated.
16. Record of Herbette's conversation with Tumanov, torgpred in Paris, and Louis Kieffer's (assistant commercial attaché) conversation with Danishevsky, director of Eksportles (Soviet timber exporters), 21.1.30: ibid.
17. Speech at the opening of a British section of the Soviet chamber of commerce for the West (German, US and Japanese sections had existed for over a year), 14.4.30 – Helleu (Moscow) to Briand (Paris), 15.4.30: ibid.
18. The proposals took the form of a letter, 21.9.27: *DVP SSSR*, Vol. X, edited by I.M.Gorokhov et al. (Moscow, 1965) doc. 219 and enclosure.
19. *Moskauer Rundschau*, 20.4.30. Further comment of the same kind appeared in an editorial, "Encore un mot sur la question du traité de commerce franco-soviétique", in *Vie Economique des Soviets*, a fortnightly published by the Commissariat for Trade, 5.6.30. That these public utterances accurately reflected private concern was confirmed by the Sûreté, who appear to have had an informant within the Soviet trade mission – report, 27.6.30: *AD*, loc. cit.
20. See, inter alia, Stomonyakov's record of a conversation with Herbette, 8.8.30: *DVP SSSR*, vol. XIII, doc. 284.
21. Herbette (Moscow) to Paris, 26.7.30: *AD*, loc. cit.; for Litvinov's record of the conversation: *DVP SSSR*, op. cit., doc. 271.
22. News that Hertzfeld had begun the seizure reached the Narkomindel on the 30 July, whereupon Stomonyakov (Litvinov being on holiday), in informing Herbette of this news, told him of the disturbing effect it was producing in Moscow; the question being asked was whether Soviet operations in France would be able to continue or whether it was not inevitable that they would be terminated "automatically" – Herbette (Moscow) to Paris, 30.7.30: *AD*, loc. cit.; for Stomonyakov's record of the conversation: *DVP SSSR*, op. cit., doc. 276.
23. A further conversation between Herbette and Stomonyakov took a similar form, and whilst firmly insisting that there was no way Hertzfeld would be paid, he also stressed that the Soviets had not yet taken action to cease trading. They would wait and see — Herbette (Moscow) to Paris, 8.8.30: *AD*, loc. cit.; for Stomonyakov's record of the conversation: *DVP SSSR*, op. cit., doc. 284.
24. Note in the Quai d'Orsay files, "from a correspondent", 15.9.30: *AD*, loc. cit. The Hertzfeld affair did not finally end to Soviet advantage until the 24 July 1931, when the French judiciary found against the plaintiff. The coincidence between this decision and the detente in relations with the USSR, combined with rumours that some jurors involved in the case had based their position originally on ideological grounds, suggests that more than points of law were involved in the judgement. For the rumours concerning bias — Stomonyakov's confidential statement to Herbette 8.8.30: *DVP SSSR*, op. cit. doc. 284.

25. Memorandum, 8.8.30: *AD*, loc. cit.
26. Memorandum by the Direction des affaires politiques et commerciales, EUROPE, 11.8.30: ibid.
27. Briand (Paris) to Herbette (Moscow), 10.9.30: ibid.
28. The claims by the French and the counter-claims by the Russians leave one bewildered as to the truth about Soviet dumping. The French claim was that between July and October the Soviets systematically dumped agricultural produce on the French market. One instance was that of prime quality Russian grain sold at 65 francs a quintal in Marseilles, as against 80 francs for an inferior grade sold on the world market — Berthelot (Paris) to Herbette (Moscow), 3.10.30: ibid. The Russians, however, countered that Soviet prices were above those of countries like Romania, as was noted in the *Bulletin des Halles* (Paris), 13.10.30, quoted in an aide-mémoire presented by Dovgalevsky to the French Government, 14.10.30: *AD*, loc. cit., and *DVP SSSR*, op. cit., doc. 354. In retrospect two points seem evident. Firstly, with the Hertzfeld case souring Franco-Soviet commercial relations, the Russians had no incentive to tread warily when setting prices for exports to France, provided they could reap enough foreign exchange in return. Secondly, whereas the overall political climate favoured action against the USSR, it could not be expected that the government would listen to proposals for a boycott of produce from an allied country also engaged in dumping, like Romania.
29. Views of the Agricultural Ministry representative, put to a meeting (no date given) held in the office of Elbel, directeur des accords commerciaux et de l'information économique at the Ministry of Commerce and Industry — Berthelot (Paris) to Léger (Geneva), 30.9.30: *AD*, loc. cit.
30. Letter, 6.10.30, from Elbel to the directeur des affaires politiques et commerciales, EUROPE, at the Quai d'Orsay: ibid. This was written in response to an article entitled "Frankreich macht den Anfang mit praktischen Gegenmassnahmen", which appeared in the *Danziger Neueste Nachrichten*, and was referred to in *Izvestiya*, 26.9.30. The article claimed to have originated in an interview with Elbel, which the latter strenuously denied, but the substance of the article does not conflict with the contents of his letter on any major point.
31. Herbette (Moscow) to Paris, 2.10.30: *AD*, loc. cit.; Litvinov's account omits any mention of this: *DVP SSSR*, op. cit., doc. 333. However, it is clear from other references to this in later correspondence that Herbette's record of the conversation is accurate: Litvinov (Moscow) to Dovgalevsky (Paris), 5.10.30: ibid., doc. 342. Berthelot dismissed the idea out of hand — Berthelot (Paris) to Herbette (Moscow), 3.10.30: *AD*, loc. cit.
32. *DVP SSSR*, op. cit., doc. 354. This followed a discussion in Moscow on the 10th, leading to the despatch of instructions to Dovgalevsky on the following day, stressing France's role as the self-appointed leader of a projected anti-Soviet bloc: ibid., p. 821.
33. Dovgalevsky (Paris) to Krestinsky (Moscow), 15.10.30: ibid., doc. 357.
34. Peretti (Brussels) to Paris, 21.10.30: *AD*, loc. cit.
35. Editorial, "Antisovetskaya 'agrarnaya' makhinatsiya No. 4", *Pravda*, 20.10.30.
36. The démenti was prompted by a United Press release in Italy to the effect that Turkey, also in Flandin's itinerary, had declined a French proposal to

join in an economic boycott of the USSR – Berthelot (Paris) to embassies in Rome, Ankara and Moscow, 3.11.30: *AD*, 1055.

37. Charles-Roux (Prague) to Paris, 10.10.30: ibid., 1054.
38. As note 35. The Soviet decree was issued by Sovnarkom, 20.10.30: *DVP SSSR*, op. cit., doc. 362.
39. Herbette (Moscow) to Paris, 22.10.30: *AD*, loc. cit.
40. Dovgalevsky (Paris) to Krestinsky (Moscow), 24.10.30: *DVP SSSR*, op. cit., doc. 365.
41. Krestinsky (Moscow) to Dovgalevsky (Paris), 6.11.30: ibid., doc. 386.
42. Herbette (Moscow) to Briand (Paris), 28.10.30: *AD*, loc. cit.

CHAPTER 5 ATTEMPTS TO COUNTER THE THREAT FROM FRANCE

1. Ovey (Moscow) to Henderson (London), 28.7.31: *DBFP*, op. cit., doc. 141.
2. E.H.Carr, *Foundations*, vol. 3, no. I, pp. 104–18.
3. *Izvestiya*, 26.7.30.
4. Moskvich, "Eshche raz razoruzhenie", ibid., 30.9.30.
5. *DVP SSSR*, vol. XIII, doc. 385.
6. Draft resolution, 13.11.30: ibid., doc. 402.
7. Interview given 28.11.30: ibid., doc. 427.
8. Lunacharsky took charge of the delegation after Litvinov's departure. For the declaration: *50 Let Bor'by SSSR za Razoruzhenie: Sbornik Dokumentov*, edited by K.V.Novikov et al. (Moscow, 1967) doc. 40.
9. See ch. 2, note 8.
10. Grandi's record of a conversation with Curtius, the German Foreign Minister, at Geneva, 25.1.31: *DDI*, vol. X, ed. R.Moscati et al. (Rome, 1978) doc. 36.
11. Germany was in fact the first European Power to grant full recognition to the Bolshevik regime.
12. Quoted by Renzo de Felice, *Mussolini il duce: I, Gli anni del consenso 1929–1936* (Turin, 1974) p. 371.
13. For example, Karakhan's record of a conversation with China's Vice-Minister for Foreign Affairs, 24.8.31: *DVP SSSR*, vol. XIV, doc. 248. These comments were to become more frequent after Hitler's accession to power (1933).
14. Paolo Spriano, *Storia del Partito comunista italiano: II, Gli anni della clandestinità* (Turin, 1969) p. 352.
15. Litvinov's record of a conversation with Italy's chargé d'affaires, Persico, 5.7.30: *DVP SSSR*, vol. XIII, doc. 244.
16. Persico (Moscow) to Rome, 3.9.30: *ASD*, Russia (1930), pacco 1558.
17. Stomonyakov's record of a conversation with Herbette, 3.9.30: *DVP SSSR*, op. cit., doc. 306.
18. Grandi's record of his discussions with Litvinov, 23.11.30: *DDI*, vol. IX, doc. 398.
19. Grandi's account of his meeting with Litvinov, which took place on the 24 November, 26.11.30: ibid., doc. 411.
20. Guariglia (director-general for Europe, the Levant and Africa) to Grandi, 26.6.30: ibid., doc. 115.

21. Grandi (Geneva) to Mussolini (Rome), 21.1.31: *DDI*, vol. x (Rome, 1978) doc. 26.

22. As note 19.

23. Grandi's account of events at Geneva, prepared for Mussolini, 2.2.31: *DDI*, vol. x, doc. 26.

24. See note 21.

25. See note 23.

26. See note 21.

27. Minute appended to Grandi (Geneva) to Mussolini (Rome) 21.1.31: ibid.

28. Litvinov (Moscow) to Sokol'nikov (London), 3.2.31: *DVP SSSR*, vol. xiv, doc. 37.

29. Krestinsky's record of a conversation with Attolico, the new Italian ambassador, 26.1.31: ibid., doc. 27.

30. The Soviet Government received its invitation on the 23 January and delayed replying for a fortnight, evidently as a result of disagreements within the leadership: ibid., doc. 39.

31. 8.3.31: ibid., doc. 73.

32. Ibid., doc. 162.

33. Ibid., doc. 163.

34. Litvinov (Geneva) to Moscow, 23.5.31: ibid., doc. 167.

35. B. Sh. (probably Boris Shtein, head of the Narkomindel's Central European department) "Evropeiskaya komissiya", *Mirovoe Khozyaistvo i Mirovaya Politika*, no. 5 (1931) pp. 3–8.

36. Ovey (Moscow) to Henderson (London), 30.6.31: *DBFP*, op. cit., doc. 138.

37. Attolico (Moscow) to Rome, 22.2.31: *ASD*, URSS (1931) 1, 1.4.

38. *DDI*, op. cit., doc. 99.

39. Note by Mussolini, dated sometime towards the end of February 1931: ibid., doc. 96.

40. Editorial, "Franko-ital'yanskoe morskoe soglashenie", *Izvestiya*, 5.3.31. One Soviet commentator recalled regretfully that "naval rivalry between France and Italy has, in the course of recent years, been an important political factor, occupying an increasingly prominent place in the range of imperialist contradictions" –L. Ivanov, "Franko-ital'yanskoe soglashenie", *Mirovoe Khozyaistvo i Mirovaya Politika*, no. 4 (1931) pp. 72–87.

41. *Vneshnyaya Torgovlya*, op. cit.

42. Editorial, "'Predstavlenie' mistera fisha", *Ekonomicheskaya Zhizn'*, 12.8.30. Representative Hamilton Fish Jr, chaired a committee investigating Communist propaganda, established under House resolution 220 on the 22 May 1930.

43. See p. 38.

44. This irritated the British Government, amongst others. On the 1 July 1931 the Cabinet decided to authorise negotiations with the German Government on a gentleman's agreement to bring German credit terms to Russia in line with those of Britain: *FO* 371/15622. This attempt eventually met with failure: *FO* 371/15600.

45. The Narkomindel's annoyance at this interference is evident from the documents – Krestinsky (Moscow) to Khinchuk (Berlin), 8.1.31: *DVP SSSR*, op. cit., doc. 5.

46. There is some confusion over the composition of the delegation. The German Foreign Ministry record contradicts the Soviet list obtained by the

Foreign Office: *AA* 72/3, B. 27, 9, D 562031, and *FO* 371/15224.

47. Moskwitsch, "DIE DEUTSCHE INDUSTRIELLE DELEGATION", *Moskauer Rundschau*, 1.3.31. Edited by Otto Pohl, this weekly had a regular section on its front page entitled "*Die Weltpolitik in der Sowjetmeinung*", of which this was one example.

48. For the progress of the visit – Krestinsky (Moscow) to Khinchuk (Berlin) 6.3.31: *DVP SSSR*, op. cit., doc. 70; *Izvestiya*, 10.3.31; and Krestinsky (Moscow) to Khinchuk (Berlin), 10.3.31: *DVP SSSR*, op. cit., doc. 79.

49. Ibid., doc. 114.

50. *Izvestiya*, 24.4.31; also Jur, "DIE POLITIK DER ZWECKMAESSIGKEIT", *Moskauer Rundschau*, 26.4.31.

51. *Izvestiya*, 29.7.31.

52. "K PERVOMU AVGUSTA: Razvernem shire boevoi front", *Kommunisticheskii Internatsional*, no. 19–20 (20.7.30) pp. 13–16.

53. "Podgotovka pokhoda protiv SSSR i germanskii imperializm", ibid., no. 8 (20.3.30) pp. 3–9.

54. Issue cited in note 52.

55. A. F – I, "Mezhdunarodny den' protiv imperialisticheskoi voiny i zadachi pechati", ibid., pp. 79–82.

56. L. Al'fred, "Protiv ravnodushiya v voprose o voennoi opasnosti", ibid., pp. 40–7.

57. Editorial by Florimond Bonte, "L'Immonde Campagne D'Excitations Antisoviétiques", *l'Humanité*, 1.2.30.

58. "L'Animateur de la Coalition Antisoviétique Vient Précipiter L'Offensive", ibid., 1.4.30.

59. "La Légende du 'dumping' prépare l'agression armée", ibid., 10.10.30.

60. Editorial by Florimond BONTE, "Les mesures gouvernementales antisoviétiques: UN COUP DIRECT CONTRE LES TRAVAILLEURS", ibid., 13.10.30.

61. These criticisms were published by the PCF in a pamphlet: *Le Parti communiste français devant l'Internationale* (Paris, 1931); see also *XI Plenum IKKI: Stenograficheskii Otchet*, I (Moscow, 1932) pp. 202–3.

CHAPTER 6   THE PLACE OF GERMANY IN SOVIET POLICY: 1930–31

1. Ovey (Moscow) to Henderson (London), 27.7.31: *DBFP*, op. cit., doc. 140.

2. Quoted in E.H.Carr, *The Interregnum 1923–1924* (London, 1960) p. 182.

3. "Il movimento nazional-socialista in Germania", unsigned, Berlin, 3.1.31: *DDI*, op. cit., doc. 2.

4. Memorandum by Sir R. Vansittart, 1.5.30: *DBFP*, series 1A, vol. VII, edited by W.N.Medlicott *et al.* (London, 1975) appendix.

5. R. Gerber, "Noveishii etap germanskogo fashizma i zadachi KPG", *Kommunisticheskii Internatsional*, no. 5 (20.2.30) pp. 19–30.

6. Martynov, "Zagnivayushchii kapitalizm i fashizatsiya burzhuaznogo gosudarstva", ibid., pp. 31–46.

7. The results were announced on the 23 June. The SPD and KPD held their

own, but the Nazis received 376,724 as against the 133,958 votes they obtained in 1929. They now had 14 seats in the Landtag.

8. *XVI S"ezd VKP (B): Stenograficheskii Otchet* (Moscow, 1931) p. 419.

9. Ibid., pp. 17–57.

10. On the 14 June 1930 the Soviet and German Governments issued a joint communiqué expressing their resolve to settle any differences which arose "in the spirit of the Rapallo treaty" and concluding with the assertion that the differences between the two systems "must not be an obstacle to future fruitful development of their friendly relations": *DVP SSSR*, vol. XIII, doc. 221.

11. Editorial, "Kompartiya Germanii v bor'be s natsional-fashizmom", *Pravda*, 17.8.30. KPD notable Fritz Heckert argued that the breach within the National Socialist Party between Otto Strasser and the Hitler leadership could not but have an unfavourable effect on Nazi electoral prospects: editorial, "§ 48 v deistvii", ibid., 20.7.30.

12. Editorial, "Narastanie revolyutsionnogo krizisa v Germanii", ibid., 16.9.30.

13. "Franko-germanskoe sblizhenie vredno dlya Germanii", ibid., 22.9.30.

14. "Usloviya franko-germanskogo voennogo soyuza", ibid., 28.10.30.

15. A.E., "DIE RUECKKEHR TARDIEUS", *Moskauer Rundschau*, 1.2.31.

16. Hoesch (Paris) to Berlin, 23.2.31: *AA* K936/K240603-5.

17. Wladimir d'Ormesson, "Le desarroi de l'Allemagne: la collaboration nécessaire de la France et des États-Unis", *l'Europe Nouvelle*, no. 678, (7.2.31) pp. 167–71; see also *Pravda*, 8.2.31.

18. There is some confusion about who made the initial approach. Dr. Weingartner in his *Stalin und der Aufstieg Hitlers. Die Deutschland-politik die Sowjetunion und die Kommunistische Internationale 1929–1934* (Berlin, 1970) p. 65, attributes the initiative to ambassador Dirksen, and the latter's own record of the conversation certainly conveys this impression – Dirksen (Moscow) to Berlin, 6.2.31: *AA* Bd. 27, 2860/D562018. However, Litvinov, in his account (which is more detailed) makes clear that it was he who made the initiative: *DVP SSSR*, vol. XIV, doc. 41.

19. Litvinov (Moscow) to Khinchuk (Berlin), 23.3.31: ibid., doc. 99.

20. This offer was made after a discussion in the Politburo, evidently on the 24th – Litvinov (Moscow) to Khinchuk (Berlin), 25.3.31: ibid., doc. 101.

21. Ibid., doc. 73.

22. Litvinov's record of a conversation with Herbette, 10.3.31: ibid., doc. 78. This was followed by an "Unofficial" approach to Beaumarchais by two Soviet delegates to a conference in Rome, who stressed that the time had come to improve Franco-Soviet relations and suggested a commercial convention or modus vivendi — Beaumarchais (Rome) to Paris, 2.4.31: *AD*, loc. cit.

23. Soviet diplomats were hamstrung by the trial which took place in November 1930 under the glare of Soviet publicity: see, for example, "Incendiaries: On the Trial of the Counter-Revolutionary 'Industrial Party' in the Soviet Union", on the front page of *International Press Correspondence*, vol. 10 (20.11.30) no. 52. All they could do to moderate its pernicious effect was to ensure that the accusations made against French officials and politicians were restricted to closed sessions. This news accompanied Litvinov's reply to Berthelot's protest, 1.12.30: *DVP SSSR*, op. cit., doc. 431. When the Soviet

court then implicated two members of the French embassy, Georges-Picot and Kieffer, this was communicated to Briand via Dovgalevsky –Litvinov (Moscow) to Dovgalevsky (Paris), 16.12.30: ibid., doc. 461. Since Georges-Picot was already safely returned to France, the French only jibbed at Kieffer's removal, which they finally agreed to in the spring of 1931, whilst simultaneously insisting on his innocence. Given that the two delegates who approached Beaumarchais in Rome (see note 22 above) claimed that the Soviet Government had been misled by forged documents incriminating the French, it would appear that the trial was entirely bogus with respect to the involvement of these diplomats in any of the plots that were revealed.

24. "L'URSS et les 'Puissances capitalistes'" — Note by the Direction des affaires politiques et commerciales, 26.3.31: *AD*, loc. cit.
25. "Avstro-germanskaya tamozhennaya uniya", *Izvestiya*, 24.3.31.
26. Editorial, "Na putyakh k evropeiskoi konferentsii", *Pravda*, 31.3.31.
27. Berthelot's record of his conversation with Dovgalevsky, 20.4.31: *AD*, loc. cit.; Dovgalevsky's own record is summarised in Dovgalevsky (Paris) to Moscow, 20.4.31: *DVP SSSR*, op. cit., doc. 118.
28. Dovgalevsky (Paris) to Krestinsky (Moscow), 21.4.31: ibid., doc. 119. There is no trace of Berthelot's indiscretions in his own account of the conversation.
29. An acid correspondence between the two departments of state can be followed in *AD*, loc. cit.
30. Dovgalevsky (Paris) to Litvinov (Moscow), 3.5.31: *DVP SSSR*, op. cit., doc. 148.
31. Litvinov's record of his conversation with Briand, 26.5.31: ibid., doc. 169.
32. Ibid., doc. 191.
33. *The Times*, 15.6.31. The Russians saw this as "SOMETHING NEW in official explanations for the USA's position on the issue of debts and reparations": *Pravda*, 16.6.31.
34. The Soviets immediately called on all Communist Parties, and particularly the Communist Parties of Germany, France and the USA, to expose this "new plan for 'the salvation' of Germany" as a means by which German workers would be further repressed — Editorial, "Novy plan 'spaseniya' germanskogo kapitalizma", *Pravda*, 23.6.31.
35. K. Radek, "Posle vystupleniya Guvera", *Izvestiya*, 10.7.31.
36. Editorial, "Krizis germanskogo kapitalizma", *Pravda*, 15.7.31.
37. Quoted in W.E.Scott, *Alliance Against Hitler: The Origins of the Franco-Soviet Pact* (London, 1962) p. 20.
38. Ibid., pp. 24–5.
39. Information from the Afghan Prime Minister (16 May) and Foreign Minister (18 May) – Maconachie (Kabul) to Henderson (London), 19.5.31: *FO* 371/15548.
40. Report on "The Situation in the Central Asiatic Military District", by T.C.E.Barstow, Major, offg. DDME, 25.5.31: ibid.
41. *DVP SSSR*, op. cit., doc. 190. Ratification followed on the 22 August (Kabul) and the 5 September (Moscow).
42. W. Petrin, "Der Sowjet-Afghanische Pakt", *Moskauer Rundschau*, 19.7.31.
43. Front page article entitled "Londonskii zagovor", *Pravda*, 22.7.31.
44. Quoted in *Pravda*, 23.7.31.

45. An account of this episode, based on KPD archives, appears in the East German history: *Geschichte der deutschen Arbeiterbewegung*, vol. 4 (Berlin, 1966) pp. 300–2. In his speech to the XII plenum of the Comintern exceutive, Pyatnitsky referred to the fact that "the leadership of the KPD" had come out against participation in the referendum, but that "the central committee together with the Comintern" jointly reached a different conclusion later: *Bol'shevik* no. 20 (1.11.32) pp. 19–29.

46. Neumann, "Osadkoe polozhenie v Germanii", *Pravda*, 31.3.31. This was an opinion shared by Comintern apparatchiks. At the XI plenum of the Comintern executive on the 8 April 1931, Martynov stated that:

> If several months ago it was possible to say that the National Socialists are the carriers of this Fascist danger then at the present moment the carrier of the Fascist danger is the Brüning Government or, as the government is described by our Communist Party, "the government responsible for introducing Fascist dictatorship", and its chief assistant in this affair is at present German social democracy.

– *XI Plenum IKKI: Stenograficheskii Otchet. Vypusk II*, pp. 67–8.

47. For Knorin's obsession with "social-Fascism" (Social Democracy) which led him to underestimate the significance of National Socialism: B.M.Leibzon and K.K.Shirinya, *Povorot v Politike Kominterna* (Moscow, 1975) pp. 101–2.

48. The British ambassador's record of a conversation with Litvinov, containing a reference to a previous discussion with Krestinsky (an account of which has not been found) — Ovey (Moscow) to Henderson (London), 26.7.31: *DBFP*, Second Series, vol. VII, doc. 139.

49. *Pravda*, 24.7.31.

50. "Itogi krasnogo plebistsita", ibid., 20.8.31.

51. Nomad, "Der Volksentscheid in Preussen", *Moskauer Rundschau*, 16.8.31.

52. For the text of the pact – Dovgalevsky (Paris) to Moscow, 10.8.31: *DVP SSSR*, op. cit., doc. 229.

53. Dovgalevsky (Paris) to Moscow, 23.9.31: ibid., doc. 273.

54. Surits (Ankara) to Moscow, 19.11.30: ibid., vol. XIII, doc. 411.

55. The published Soviet documents are silent concerning Antonov-Ovseenko's activities at this stage. This information in the text comes from Laroche (Warsaw) to Paris, 23.12.30: *AD*, 959. The only reference in Soviet materials is to Surits' conversations in Ankara: Surits (Ankara) to Moscow, 27.11.30: *DVP SSSR*, op. cit., doc. 426.

56. One factor that might partly account for the change in the Polish position was the uncertainty prior to the elections (16-23 November) which forced the Foreign Ministry to consider options which the parties further to the Right might choose; for, as we have seen in relation to the crisis in Polish-Soviet relations in the spring of 1930, the Dmowski camp were more preoccupied with the German than the Soviet threat. In the event the regime had no problem in defeating the opposition at the polls.

57. *DVP SSSR*, vol. XIV, doc. 247.

58. This is what Berthelot told the polpred in mid-February 1932 – Dovgalevsky (Paris) to Moscow, 18.2.32: ibid., vol. XV, doc. 83.

59. Memorandum, 14.1.32: *AD*, 1057.
60. D. Kitsikis, "La Grèce et le projet Briand d'Union européenne due 1er mai 1930", *Revue d'Histoire Moderne et Contemporaine*, vol. XII, 1965, pp. 203–18. I have been unable to trace the French record of this conversation in the archives – much went up in smoke in the panic of 1940.
61. Nemo, "Vokrug franko-germanskogo voennogo soyuza", *Kommunisticheskii Internatsional*, nos 33–4 (1931) pp. 35–43.
62. Editorial, "Pravitel'stvenny krizis v Germanii", *Pravda*, 11.10.31.
63. Litvinov (Geneva) to Moscow, 6.9.31: *DVP SSSR*, op. cit., doc. 261.

CHAPTER 7   THE MANCHURIAN CRISIS: 1931

1. For a comprehensive account of the Japanese decision to occupy Manchuria: S.Ogata, *Defiance in Manchuria* (Berkeley, 1964).
2. The Politburo's special commission on the CER in March 1926 had emphasised the strategic importance of the railroad. A copy of the report was subsequently published by Trotsky in *Byulleten' Oppozitsii*, nos 3–4 (5.9.29). Stalin himself appears to have been sceptical of its value. According to Besedovsky, who served in Tokyo as chargé d'affaires, Stalin in 1927 suggested selling the CER as a means of exacerbating the differences between the various capitalist Powers in the Far East – G.Z.Besedovsky, *Na Putyakh k Termidoru* (Paris, 1930) pp. 137–8. This would appear to conflict with the USSR's resolute defence of the CER in 1929, but there was a major difference between selling the railway to a willing customer and surrendering it under assault from the Chinese. The Red Army's action was as much motivated by the need to teach the Kuomintang (and the West) that the USSR would defend its possessions with force if necessary.
3. Alec Nove, op. cit., p. 177.
4. V. Dushen'kin, *Proletarskii Marshal* (Moscow, 1973) p. 112. At the 5 Amur regional party conference on the 11 May 1930 Blyukher, a member of the *Dal'kraikom* (Far Eastern regional committee), stressed the need to create the Far East's own military-economic base: Z.Sh. Yanguzov, *Osobaya Krasnoznamennaya Dal'nevostochnaya Armiya na Strazhe Mira i Bezopasnosti SSSR (1929–1938gg.)* (Blagoveshchensk, 1970) p. 111.
5. "From a correspondent" (this can mean the Foreign Office, though no trace could be found in the archives), *The Times*, 20.11.30. Russian emigré literature, often highly dubious as a source, confirms this. One writer, who evidently served in the army, but whose credentials can not easily be checked, claims that from 1930 to 1931 Gamarnik (referred to in Appendix 1) had to take command of the Far Eastern army, and that Blyukher was popularly known as "the Tsar of Siberia", which certainly could not have pleased Stalin: A.Svetlanin, "Dal'nevostochny zagovor (Zagovor Krutova, dal'nevostochnaya chistka i Blyukher)", *Posev*, 27.4.52.
6. *The Times*, 22.11.30 and 25.11.30.
7. This is what reached the Foreign Office early in June:

        according to a usually well-informed source, there has been trouble in the army. I am credibly informed that General Blucher, who returned from the Chinese frontier last year, has been for some months under arrest; that twenty-six members of the General Staff have been executed, and, what is more significant, if true, that no fewer than 300 members of the GPU have met the same fate.

It was said to have followed the planning of a putsch for the 15 May 1931 – Ovey (Moscow) to London, 2.6.31: *FO* 371/15601. This may well be an exaggeration, but coming as it did just before a thorough purge of the Soviet high command, lends credence to the idea that some sort of confrontation had taken place between military leaders and the Party leadership. On the 11 June Uborevich was dismissed from his post as deputy chairman of the Revvoensovet and sent to command the Byelorussian military district. Tukhachevsky replaced him in Moscow. Chief of Staff Shaposhnikov was replaced by Yegorov and sent to command the Volga military district. Member of the Revvoensovet and naval chief Muklevich was replaced by Orlov and member of the Revvoensovet and air force chief Baranov was replaced by Alksnis and appointed to the presidium of Vesenkha: "Letopis stroitel'stva sovetskikh vooruzhennykh sil 1931 god", *Voenno-Istoricheskii Zhurnal*, no. 4 (April 1977) pp. 122–3.

8. *Ibid.*, no. 2 (1977) pp. 114–15.
9. In his speech of thanks Blyukher stated: "I assure the Party and the Government that I will also henceforth be a fighter for the Party and the working class": Dushen'kin, loc. cit. "The tour of inspection of Voroshiloff, the Commissar for War, in the Far East resulted in a reconciliation between the leaders of the Communist Party in Moscow and the Commander of the Far Eastern Army, General Galents [*sic*], who had fallen from favour": *The Times*, 11.8.31. Blyukher used the name "Galin" when working as military adviser to the Kuomintang in the twenties.
10. "Tov. Voroshilov na dal'nevostochnom fronte sotsialisticheskogo stroitel'stva", *Izvestiya*, 19.8.31.
11. *International Military Tribunal Far East (IMTFE): Japanese Trials 27 May –4 June 1947*, pp. 23 238 and 23 258.
12. The document was entitled "Views Concerning our Imperial National Defense against the USSR" and was produced by the Prosecution in evidence: ibid., pp. 23 213–225. It was quoted in *Izvestiya* on the 4 March 1932, along with another telegram implicating Hirota, the Japanese ambassador (see below).
13. Karakhan's record of his conversation with Hirota, 19.9.31: *DVP SSSR*, vol. xiv, doc. 269.
14. Litvinov's record of his conversation with Hirota, 22.9.31: ibid. doc. 271.
15. Karakhan's record of his conversation with Mo, 23.9.31: ibid., doc. 272. Litvinov repeated this to Strang, 24.9.31: ibid., doc. 275.
16. Negotiations opened on the 11 October 1930, following an agreement on the 22 December 1929. Karakhan represented the USSR at the talks. For the 1929 agreement: *DVP SSSR*, vol. xii, doc. 390; for the opening of negotiations: ibid., vol. xiii, doc. 352.
17. "Voennaya okkupatsiya Manchzhurii", *Pravda*, 25.9.31.

18. *The Times*, 25.9.31.

19. Editorial, "Interventsiya v Manchzhurii i manevry imperialistov", *Izvestiya*, 26.9.31.

20. Editorial, "Bor'ba iz-za manchzhurskii dobychi", *Pravda*, 18.10.31.

21. P. Mif, "Yaponskii imperialism i okkupatsiya Manchzhurii", *Bol'shevik*, no. 22 (30.11.31) pp. 30–41.

22. Editorial, "Cherny den' mezhdunarodnogo imperializma", *Pravda*, 22.9.31; also, editorial, "Klassovye boi v Anglii", ibid., 9.10.31; and "Ot oppozitsii – k revolyutsionnoi klassovoi bor'be (polozhenie v Anglii)", *Kommunisticheskii Internatsional*, no. 28 (10.10.31) pp. 2–11.

23. N., "DIE OKKUPATION DER MANDSCHUREI", *Moskauer Rundschau*, 27.9.31.

24. Dated 29.12.31, and originally published by the CCP in 1932–3, republished in Taiwan by Warren Kuo, *Analytical History of the Chinese Communist Party* (Second edition, Taipei, 1968) ch. 18, appendix 1.

25. Ibid., pp. 372–3.

26. Reprinted in Aki, "Grabitel'skaya voina yaponskogo imperializma v Kitae i antivoennaya bor'ba yaponskogo proletariata", *Kommunisticheskii Internatsional*, no. 4 (10.2.31) pp. 40–50.

27. "Polozhenie Yaponii i zadachi KPYa", ibid., nos 8–9 (30.3.32) pp. 3–14.

28. Sen-Katayama and Tokita, "Okkupatsiya Manchzhurii i bor'ba yaponskogo proletariata protiv imperializma", *Pravda*, 5.10.31.

29. "Yaponskii imperializm i kharakter yaponskoi revolyutsii", *Mirovoe Khozyaistvo i Mirovaya Politika*, no. 6 (1932) pp. 3–14.

30. Karakhan cabled polpred Okhtin in Outer Mongolia, warning him to expect "provocative activities" on the Mongolian border with China, organised by the Whites, 24.9.31: *DVP SSSR*, vol. XIV, doc. 276. Indeed, according to the French consul in Harbin secret meetings were taking place at the Japanese military mission in the city at which the resources of the Russian emigrés were being considered with a view to their deployment against the Soviets – Reynaud (Harbin) to Wilden (Peking), 5.10.31: *AD*, SDN, 1917–40, 320. By the spring of 1932 the Japanese had formed cavalry units composed of Mongols and Buryats hostile to Soviet rule – Reynaud (Harbin) to Wilden (Peking), 27.4.32: ibid.

31. Litvinov's record of his conversation with Hirota, 2.10.31: ibid., doc. 288.

32. Hirota delivered the ultimatum on the 28 October. Karakhan's reply dated the 29th was published by TASS on the following day. The Soviet reply, although it contains a vigorous denial of the assertion that Soviet instructors were aiding Ma, does not attempt to deny that Ma met with a Soviet officer from Blagoveshchensk between the 12 and 13 October: ibid., doc. 320. The Russian reply left the Japanese unconvinced that the Soviets were not supplying artillery and shells to Ma via the CER, purportedly on the 21 October: ibid., p. 820. The Japanese were sure that their information on this was correct: Ogata, op. cit., p. 110; so were the French – Payart (Moscow) to Briand (Paris), 28.10.31: *AD*, op. cit., 323.

33. TASS reported the Japanese claim on the 12 November: *Izvestiya*, 14.11.31. The instruction was sent to Harbin on the same day as the TASS report reached Moscow: *DVP SSSR*, op. cit., doc. 350.

34. Ibid., doc. 335.

35. Litvinov's record of his conversation with Hirota, 14.11.31. The Commissar referred to "this unfair anti-Soviet campaign, systematically carried on by some military circles in Manchuria with the aim of complicating relations between Japan and the USSR". He also had information that the Kwantung army intended to cross the CER and paralyse its functions in the Tsitsihar region: ibid., doc. 341.
36. Ibid., doc. 385.
37. Sensitivity on this point was illustrated when an employee of Narkomput', possibly an agent provocateur, informed OGPU that Vanek, a secretary at the Czech embassy in Moscow, had suggested assassinating the Japanese ambassador as a means of provoking a war between Japan and the USSR. OGPU is said to have been informed of this on the very day of Molotov's speech to the central executive committee, and Litvinov informed polpred Arosev in Prague of this incident on the 23rd. Vanek was then declared persona non grata – Litvinov (Moscow) to Arosev (Prague), 23.12.31: ibid., doc. 390. The British ambassador reported home that Vanek had made himself extremely unpopular with the Soviet authorities by his involvement in the black market, but that he was most probably innocent of the charges laid against him – Ovey (Moscow) to Simon (London), 31.12.31: *FO* 371/16324. Other foreign missions were less certain, though sceptical of OGPU claims – Attolico (Moscow) to Rome, 30.1.32: *ASD*, URSS (1932), b.8, pac. 1.9; and Dirksen (Moscow) to Berlin, 25.12.31: *AA* 72/3, 29, 9.
38. Litvinov's account of the conversation, 31.12.31: *DVP SSSR*, op. cit., doc. 401. Yoshizawa's own account bears this out: "Yoshizawa.gaishō no Nisso fukashin jōyaku, Manshū jihen ni kansuru kaisōdan", in *Kokusai Seiji*, no. 1 (1966) pp. 105–18. Also: *IMTFE: Japanese Trials 19–26 May 1947*, pp. 22 678–81.
39. L.N.Kutakov, *Istoriya Sovetsko-Yaponskikh Diplomaticheskikh Otnoshenii* (Moscow, 1962) pp. 114–5.
40. Troyanovsky (Tokyo) to Moscow, 7.1.32: *DVP SSSR*, vol. xv, doc. 6.
41. This was the tenor of Litvinov's remarks to Ovey – Ovey (Moscow) to Simon (London), 14.1.32: *DBFP*, op. cit., doc. 147.
42. Troyanovsky's record of a conversation with Tanaka, director of the Japanese–Soviet Society, 26.1.32: *DVP SSSR*, op. cit., doc. 44.
43. The first incident of this nature occurred on the 27 January 1932 when Japanese officers and men demanded seats on a train to Harbin, and used force to obtain them. The Soviet consul in Harbin informed Moscow of this on the same day — Slavutsky (Harbin) to Moscow, 27.1.32: ibid., p. 730.
44. Karakhan (Moscow) to Slavutsky (Harbin), 28.1.32: ibid., doc. 50.
45. Karakhan (Moscow) to Slavutsky (Harbin), 2.2.32: ibid., doc. 61. See also docs. 86–7 and p. 743.
46. Slavutsky (Harbin) to Moscow, 4.2.32: ibid., doc. 66.
47. The Portsmouth treaty on the 5 September 1905 restored peaceful relations after the Russo-Japanese war. For Soviet insistence on the observance of their rights under the treaty, see Karakhan's statement to Hirota, 27.2.32, published in *Izvestiya*, 29.2.32, and reprinted in *DVP SSSR*, op. cit., doc. 100.
48. Article 2 of the Portsmouth treaty provided that both parties "refrain from taking any military measures whatsoever on the Russo-Korean frontier,

which might threaten the security of Russian or Korean territory":
Mezhdunarodnye Otnosheniya 1870–1918gg: Sbornik Dokumentov, edited
by V.M.Khvostov (Moscow, 1940) doc. 82.

49. This is the translation given by the interpreter at the Tokyo war crimes
tribunal: *IMTFE: Japanese Trials 4-10 October 1946*, pp. 7 485–6. There
the defence made much of the fact that other sections of the document were
illegible (pp. 7 452–3), yet it is curious, to say the least, that the Soviet
prosecutor did not produce the Russian intercept in evidence, given its
publication in *Izvestiya* on the 4 March 1932. I have only used the trial
translation because it reads better than the *Izvestiya* equivalent; there is no
difference in meaning.

50. Moscow was informed about the creation of Manchukuo on the 12 March
1932: *DVP SSSR*, op. cit., p. 753.

51. Karakhan (Moscow) to Slavutsky (Harbin), 22.3.32: ibid., doc. 136.

52. Ibid., p. 753.

53. The French embassy in Stockholm obtained this information from "a
reliable source" – Gaussen (Stockholm) to Paris, 15.2.32: *AD*, EUROPE,
1930–40, URSS, 1012. See also Dejean (Moscow) to Paris, 26.2.32: ibid.,
SDN, 1917–40, 334; and Dejean (Moscow) to Laval (Paris), 1.3.32: ibid.

54. Troyanovsky (Tokyo) to Moscow, 17.3.32: *DVP SSSR*, op. cit., doc. 126.

55. A rather pedestrian and uninformative account of his period in Tokyo
appears in E.I.Krutitskaya and L.S.Mitrofanova, *Polpred Aleksandr
Troyanovsky* (Moscow, 1975) pp. 54–138.

56. Troyanovsky (Tokyo) to Karakhan (Moscow), 31.3.32: *DVP SSSR*, op. cit.,
doc. 145. This news must have come as a considerable source of relief of
Karakhan, hitherto unable to leave Moscow due to the pressing urgency of
the problem faced in the Far East — Karakhan's record of a conversation
with Mo, 17.3.32: ibid., doc. 127. Krestinsky, too, was caught up in the
reconsideration of Far Eastern policy. He told the Estonian Minister on the 3
March that because of the distraction of the Far East, he had no time for the
negotiations on a non-aggression pact; Litvinov's hurried return to Moscow,
arriving on the 2 March and leaving the following day for Geneva, also
points to the overwhelming predominance of the Far Eastern crisis at this
time over all other matters – Dejean (Moscow) to Paris, 4.3.32: *AD*,
EUROPE 1930–40, URSS, 1012.

CHAPTER 8   THE THREAT FROM JAPAN TAKES PRIORITY

1. S.Zakharov *et al.*, *Tikhookeanskii Flot* (Moscow, 1966) pp. 118–21.

2. Japanese estimates were as follows:

> September 1931
> > sharpshooter divisions   6
> > cavalry brigades   2
> September 1932
> > sharpshooter divisions   8
> > cavalry divisions   1

brigades	11
aircraft	200
tanks	250

IMTFE: Japanese Trials 27 May–4 June 1947, pp. 23 555–6. Other estimates are less detailed. Lt Col. De Ferrari, the Italian military attaché, put the total figure at not less than 100 000 – Attolico (Moscow) to Rome, 15.3.32: *ASD*, URSS, (1932) b.5, pac. 1.1. The Polish military attaché, on the other hand, estimated 200 000. The massive difference in the size of the estimate may be accounted for partly by the inclusion of paramilitary forces in the Polish figure, and also by an understandable tendency on the part of the Poles to err on the side of exaggeration where Red Army numbers were concerned. The British, lacking an attaché in Moscow, relied on these Polish figures – Ovey (Moscow) to Simon (London), 28.3.32: *DBFP*, op. cit., vol. x, edited by Medlicott et al. (London, 1969) doc. 149.

3. *Istoriya Vtoroi Mirovoi Voiny 1939–1945*, edited by A. Grechko et al. (Moscow, 1973) vol. 1, p. 110.
4. "The Results of the First Five-Year Plan", Report Delivered on the 7 January 1933: Stalin, op. cit., pp. 182–3.
5. Strang (Moscow) to Simon (London), 8.4.32: DBFP, op. cit., doc. 184.
6. UK delegation (Geneva) to London, 26.4.32: ibid., doc. 270 (enclosure); also, for further evidence, see Attolico (Moscow) to Rome, 15.3.32, as cited in 2. The Soviet budget deliberately concealed the real increase in defence spending: J. Cooper, "Defence Production and the Soviet Economy 1929–1941", *CREES Discussion Papers*, Series SIPS, no. 3 (Birmingham, 1976) pp. 33–41.
7. Tabriz Political Diary, no. 5 (May 1932); no. 6 (June 1932), and no. 10 (October 1932) – *FO* 371/16339.
8. Strang (Moscow) to Simon (London), 14.8.32: *FO* 371/16322.
9. CCP program for struggle, 2.2.32: Kuo, op. cit., ch. 18, appendix 2.
10. Ibid., pp. 375–6.
11. Ibid., p. 377.
12. CC CCP Directive to Kiangsu Provincial Committee, 18.3.32: ibid., pp. 374–5.
13. Van Min, "Uglublenie revolyutsionnogo krizisa v Kitae i zadachi kitaiskoi kompartii", *Bol'shevik*, no. 5-6 (31.3.32) pp. 26–4.
14. K.K.Shirinya, *Strategiya i Taktika Kominterna v Bor'be Protiv Fashizma i Voiny (1934–1939gg)* (Moscow, 1979) p. 49.
15. Quoted from the Bulgarian Party archives by F.I.Firsov, "Georgi Dimitrov and the West European Bureau of the Comintern", in *Georgi Dimitrov: an Outstanding Militant of the Comintern* (English edition, Sofia, 1972).
16. *Iz Istorii Mezhdunarodnoi Proletarskoi Solidarnosti: Dokumenty i Materialy, Sbornik IV: Mezhdunarodnaya Proletarskaya Solidarnost' v Bor'be s Nastupleniem Fashizma (1928–1932)*, edited by G.A.Belov et al. (Moscow, 1960) doc. 174.
17. Ibid., docs. 187, 189, 193 and 195.
18. "Interventsiya protiv Manchzhurii i podgotovka bol'shoi antisovetskoi voiny", *Kommunisticheskii Internatsional*, no. 33–4 (10.12.31) pp. 3–9.
19. The concluding paragraph to Van Min's "Anti-imperialisticheskoe dvizhenie v Kitae", ibid., no. 36 (30.12.31) pp. 26–37.

20. "Mir vpolzaet v mirovuyu imperialisticheskuyu voinu", *Kommunisticheskii Internatsional*, no. 4 (10.2.32) pp. 3–9.

21. "Kommunisticheskaya pechat' v bor'be protiv voiny", ibid, pp. 51–6.

22. "Voina i blizhaishie zadachi kommunisticheskikh partii", ibid., no. 6 (29.2.32) pp. 3–9.

23. L.A., "Bor'ba protiv voennykh postavok", ibid., no. 7 (10.3.32) pp. 25–30.

24. *Iz Istorii*, doc. 118.

25. The article on "War and the Tasks of Communists" was signed with the initials G.K., in the April issue of *Die Internationale*, the KPD journal.

26. Al'fred, 'O nesvoevremennom primenenii lozunga mira", *Kommunisticheskii Internatsional*, no. 13 (10.5.32) pp. 3–8

27. Babette Gross, *WILLI MÜNZENBERG: Eine politische Biographie* (Stuttgart, 1967) pp. 236–7.

28. *IVMV*, pp. 315 and 317–18. The news was announced in *International Press Correspondence*, 26.5.32.

29. For Rolland's objections to the use of his name on the invitation without authorisation, see his letter of the 14 July 1932: Gross, op. cit., pp. 237–8.

30. Pamphlet entitled *United Front Against War: Report and Manifesto of the World Anti-War Congress at Amsterdam*, published by the British delegation (London, 1932).

31. Ibid.

32. Also published in *International Press Correspondence*, 15.9.32. The statement on this issue was as follows:

FUTILE PACIFISM

It is aware that many distinguished minds are desperately seeking to find a means of saving society by noble dreams. It is aware that there are men who offer a personal resistance to war which may draw down upon them the vengeance of capitalist laws. But it considers that in the face of the terrible challenge offered by present developments it is impossible to stop short at abstract formulas, or to confine oneself to means of resistance foredoomed to failure; notably the — unfortunately futile — sacrifice constituted by the noble attitude adopted after a declaration of war by conscientious objectors, and by all others who fling themselves individually against a collective disaster.

It hopes that the men of character and courage who preach those heroic measures and who are prepared to accept for themselves the very grave consequences of such an attitude, will join with the others in erecting, stone by stone, from the ground up, a massive collective barrier against war. Every form of opposition to this work merely helps the enemy.

33. The most significant change in the text was the omission in *Pravda* of the word "unfortunately" from the phrase about "the – unfortunately futile – sacrifice" (see above): "Manifest amsterdamskogo antivoennogo kongressa", *Pravda*, 15.9.32.

34. B. Sh., "Itogi razoruzhitel'noi komissii v svete protivorechii imperializma", *Mirovoe Khozyaistvo i Mirovaya Politika*, no. 1 (1931) pp. 17–20.

35. Dated 15.1.31: *DVP SSSR*, vol. XIV, doc. 15, originally published in *Izvestiya*, 15.1.31.

36. See, for example, Soviet irritability at Drummond's unexpected reference to the future publication by the League of Russian armaments figures (submitted to him on the 25 April 1931) – Litvinov (Moscow) to Drummond (Geneva), 19.5.31: *DVP SSSR*, op. cit., doc. 165.

37. On the 20 April 1932 the League Secretary-General wrote to Litvinov asking the Russians to co-operate with the Lytton commission, investigating the origins of the Sino-Japanese war, by allowing it to receive assistance from Soviet consuls in Manchuria. Litvinov refused (reply dated 22.4.32) – note dated Geneva, 26.4.32: *AD*, SDN, 1917–40, 338; *DVP SSSR*, op. cit., doc. 180 and enclosure.

38. Speech by Grandi: *Documents on International Affairs 1931*, edited by J.W.Wheeler-Bennett (London, 1932) p. 39.

39. This, despite the tactless manner in which Titulescu, the Romanian chairman of the League Assembly, gave the Soviets only one day's notice of the meeting to discuss the matter — Litvinov (Moscow) to Titulescu (Geneva), 21.9.31: *DVP SSSR*, op. cit., doc. 270. The USSR's conditions were reiterated in Litvinov's circular to all Soviet missions abroad dated 22.12.31: ibid., doc. 360.

40. *Documents*, op. cit., pp. 39–40.

41. *DVP SSSR*, vol. XV, doc. 75.

42. Litvinov (Geneva) to Moscow, 19.4.32: ibid., doc. 173.

43. Soviet defence expenditure was rising: see note 6.

44. The resolution was accepted by 41 delegations, with 8 abstentions and only Germany and the USSR voting against.

45. *The Memoirs of Captain Liddell Hart*, vol. 1 (London, 1965) pp. 196–7.

46. L. I–v, "Balans zhenevskogo 'razoruzheniya'", *Kommunisticheskii Internatsional*, no. 18 (30.6.32) pp. 43–53. *Izvestiya* ("Protiv sabotazha razoruzheniya", editorial, 26.7.32) and *Pravda* ("Dva itoga 'razoruzheniya'", editorial, 27.7.32), whilst critical, were much less dogmatic. By the end of the year, however, the Russians were expressing their concern that the collapse of hopes for disarmament was "indicative of the speed with which the [*sic*] imperialist antagonisms are sharpening": "The Disarmament Conference Comes to an End", a premature obituary which appeared in *Moscow Daily News*, 10.12.32.

CHAPTER 9   FAR EASTERN CRISIS: SOVIET POLICY, EUROPE, 1932

1. Report from the Soviet embassy in Berlin on Germany in 1931, 7.4.32: *DVP SSSR*, vol. XIV, p. 751.

2. Editorial, "Politika frantsuzskogo imperializma", *Pravda*, 2.12.31.

3. "Note sur les répercussions du conflit sino-japonais en Indochine" – Pasquier (Hanoi) to Paris, 28.3.32, enclosed in Colonial Ministry to Prime and Foreign Ministers, 4.5.32: *AD*, SDN, 1917–40, 333.

4. See note 10.

5. Asie-Océanie, "CONFLIT SINO-JAPONAIS", 25.2.32: source as in note 3.
6. Letter from PCF Deputies signed by Jacques Doriot, 30.10.31: ibid., 323.
7. See, for example, *The Daily Express*, 11.2.32; and for the French denial – Berthelot (Paris) to Claudel (Washington), 21.2.32: ibid., 333.
8. Rozenberg (Paris) to Rubinin (Moscow), 16.2.32: *DVP SSSR*, vol. XV, doc. 80.
9. Suggested by Leger, Berthelot's successor, on the 12 August 1932: ibid., p. 788.
10. Herriot (Paris) to de Léger (Tokyo), 15.9.32: *Documents Diplomatiques Français 1932–1939*, 1st series, vol. 1 (Paris, 1964), doc. 182 and de Lens (Tokyo) to Herriot (Paris), 23.9.32: ibid., doc. 210.
11. Ya. Volk, "Yaponiya na arene voiny i revolyutsii", *Bol'shevik*, no.7 (15.4.32) pp. 61–72.
12. Wang Ming: *XII plenum IKKI: stenograficheskii otchet*, I (Moscow, 1933) second meeting, 28.8.32.
13. Lord Tyrrell (Paris) to Sir R. Lindsay (Washington), 21.10.31: *DBFP*, 2nd series, vol. II (London, 1947) doc. 276.
14. The recollections of François-Poncet's personal assistant in Berlin – A. Bérard, *Un ambassadeur se souvient: au tempts du danger allemand* (Paris, 1976) p. 109.
15. Editorial, "Franko-germanskie peregovory i obostrenie versal'skikh protivorechii", *Pravda*, 13.11.31.
16. Editorial, "Nakanune Lozannskoi konferentsii", ibid., 14.1.32.
17. Editorial, "Manevry germanskogo sotsial-fashizma i bor'ba za proletarskii ediny front", ibid., 20.1.32.
18. Sir H. Rumbold (Berlin) to Sir J. Simon (London), 13.4.32: *DBFP*, 2nd Series, vol. III (London, 1948) doc. 98.
19. Thälmann was speaking to the Saxony regional party conference of the KPD: *Pravda*, 3.4.32.
20. Editorial, "Vybory v prusskii landtag", ibid., 26.4.32.
21. Rumbold (Berlin) to Simon (London), 1.3.32: *DBFP*, op. cit., doc. 95.
22. Sepp Shvab, "Energichnee borot'sya protiv opportunizma", *Kommunisticheskii Internatsional*, no. 5 (20.2.32).
23. "It stood to reason, he said, that there was a Bolshevist peril in a country containing 6 000 000 to 7 000 000 Communists and 4 000 000 left-wing Socialists who might easily be carried away by them, to say nothing of foreign allies to the East" – this is the only section of Hitler's interview given to foreign correspondents on the 4 December 1931 which touches on the USSR: *The Times*, 5.12.31.
24. Khinchuk (Berlin) to Krestinsky (Moscow), 28.4.32: *DVP SSSR*, vol. XV, doc. 193.
25. On the 15 April 1932 Soviet Intelligence asked its *rezident* in Rome to check whether the Italian Government was subsidising Hitler's movement. The reply was evidently positive, for on the 30 April Moscow informed him that reprisals would be taken against the Italians: they would have to buy their grain elsewhere. This and other items (including the contents of the polpred's wastepaper basket) can be found in the archives of the Italian Interior Ministry. The Italian secret police had penetrated the Soviet embassy in Rome: Ministèro Interno, Direttore Generale PS – Divisione

Affari Riservati: *Polizia Politica*, Pacco 164, Cat. M.12, Nr. 6. There is no direct indication of this in the Soviet documents, though the Italians did, in December of that year, complain that the Russians were refusing them "hard grain for macaroni" — Litvinov's record of a conversation with Attolico, 1.12.32: *DVP SSSR*, op. cit., doc. 464.

26. Rumbold (Berlin) to Sargent (London), 4.5.32: *DBFP*, op. cit., doc. 108.
27. J. Bariéty and C. Bloch, "Une tentative de réconciliation franco-allemande et son échec (1932–1933)", *Revue d'Histoire Moderne et Contemporaine*, vol. xv, July–September 1968, pp. 433–65.
28. Editorial, "Pravitel'stvenny krizis v Germanii", *Pravda*, 3.6.32.
29. Khinchuk (Berlin) to Krestinsky (Moscow), 25.6.32: *DVP SSSR*, op. cit., doc. 263.
30. Entry in Herriot's diary for the 16 June 1932: E. Herriot, *Jadis: d'une guerre à l'autre 1914–1936* (Paris, 1952) p. 322. See also the record of a conversation between M. de Laboulaye, member of the French delegation to Lausanne (and directeur adjoint des affaires politiques et commerciales) and von Bülow, member of the German delegation (and head of the Wilhelmstrasse), on the 20 June – Herriot to François-Poncet (Berlin), 20.7.32: *DDF*, op. cit., doc. 46, annexe III. In his memoirs von Papen is more reticent, referring merely to the offer of a consultative pact — Franz von Papen, *Memoirs* (London, 1952) p. 175.
31. Report from Alexander (Andrew Rothstein?) in Lausanne, dated 30.6.32:

> Amongst members of the German delegation, as elsewhere, nobody any longer tries to deny that talks about projected Franco-German 'military co-operation' took place last week between the German and French delegations.

> – *Pravda*, 1.7.32.

32. André François-Poncet, *The Fateful Years: Memoirs of a French Ambassador in Berlin 1931–1938* (New York, 1949) pp. 31–3.
33. Papen's offer to the French was never forgotten by the Russians who, according to the report of the Soviet embassy in Berlin on Germany in 1932, considered that there was no doubt at all that Papen had tried for an agreement with France, the price being a military alliance including Poland for the struggle against Bolshevism; "never before was the idea of 'a crusade' against the USSR taken with such seriousness, as in the era of the Papen Cabinet', the report added: quoted in *DVP SSSR*, vol. xv, p. 780. 780.
34. Khinchuk's record of a conversation with von Schleicher, 27.6.32: ibid., doc. 265.
35. Editorial, "Lozannskii torg", *Pravda*, 8.7.32.
36. The testimony of Jacques Duclos, a leading French Communist, then working with Dimitrov at the Comintern's West European Bureau in Berlin. Dimitrov asked Thälmann why the KPD did not declare a strike and the answer he received was that it would be very difficult, if not impossible: Zhak Dyuklo, "Zashchitnik svobody i chelovecheskogo dostoinstva", *Vospominaniya o Georgii Dimitrove* (Sofia, 1972).

37. Quoted in L.Fisher, *Russia's Road from Peace to War: Soviet Foreign Relations 1917–1941* (New York, 1969) p. 222.

38. Stomonyakov (Moscow) to Antonov-Ovseenko (Warsaw), 22.4.32: *DVP SSSR*, op. cit., doc. 183.

39. The Russians refused to acknowledge any linkage between these various negotiations, but nonetheless had to accept it as a fait accompli. For Soviet rejection of the linkage — Litvinov (Moscow) to Dovgalevsky (Paris), 15.11.31: *DVP SSSR*, vol. XIV, doc. 342. On the 4 May Dirksen told Litvinov that Pilsudski's visit to Romania was motivated by the need to persuade the Romanians to conclude a pact with the USSR — Litvinov's record of the conversation, 4.5.32: ibid., vol. XV, doc. 202; for Antonov-Ovseenko's evaluation, 7.5.32: ibid., doc. 208.

40. 21.1.32: ibid., doc. 32.

41. 5.2.32: ibid., doc. 67.

42. 4.5.32: ibid., doc. 201.

43. 6.5.32: ibid., vol. XIV, doc. 152.

44. As note 38.

45. *DVP SSSR*, vol. XV, doc. 300.

46. Editorial, "Novye uspekhi mirnoi politiki SSSR", *Pravda*, 30.7.32.

47. K. Radek, "Mezhdunarodnye protivorechiya v 1932g", *Bol'shevik*, no. 22 (30.11.32) pp. 50–64.

CHAPTER 10   A TEMPORARY SETBACK IN RELATIONS WITH BRITAIN

1. Towards the end of July 1931 Lady Astor and her companions (including George Bernard Shaw) obtained an interview with Stalin, during their stay as guests of the Soviet Government. Stalin was eager to have news of Winston Churchill, being particularly interested to know what office he was likely to hold in the event of the Conservatives regaining power. Lady Astor's disparaging remarks about Churchill as a spent force in British politics met with scepticism from Stalin, who appeared convinced that Churchill was bound to rise to the top again and would then launch a further crusade against the Soviet Union (as in 1918–19): Christopher Sykes, *NANCY: The Life of Lady Astor* (London, 1972) p. 340. Churchill's omission from the Cabinet thus removed any immediate fears on this score that Stalin may have harboured. Editorials in *Pravda* ("Makdonal'd vo glave 'natsional'nogo' pravitel'stva") and *Izvestiya* ("Pravitel'stvo spaseniya kapitalizma") on the 25 August both focused on the seeming bankruptcy of Labour rather than on any threat from Conservative participation in the new coalition.

2. Editorial, "Klassovye boi v Anglii", *Pravda*, 9.10.31. A more detailed discussion of events in Britain, along much the same lines, appeared in the Comintern journal on the following day: "Ot oppozitsii k revolyutsionnoi klassovoi bor'be (polozhenie v Anglii)", *Kommunisticheskii Internatsional*, no. 28 (10.10.31). pp. 2–11.

3. Membership reached its nadir at 2555 in November 1930, and had risen to

only 9 000 by early 1932: H. Pelling, *The British Communist Party: A Historical Profile* (London, 1958) appendix A.

4. From a speech at a Comintern meeting on the English question in December 1931, printed under the title "Uroki angliiskikh vyborov", in *Kommunisticheskii Internatsional*, no. 7 (10.3.32) pp. 12–24.

5. Conversation, 26.2.32 – Ovey (Moscow) to Simon (London), 29.2.32: *FO* 371/16322.

6. For the expression of .discontent: *Parliamentary Debates: the House of Commons*, vol. 252, col. 1679. Matters were made worse by the fact that a large proportion of the total export credits guaranteed by the British Government went to the Soviet Union: ibid., vol. 270, col. 735. For information on the passive balance of trade: *DBFP*, vol. VII, doc. 153 (enclosure); also the admission by Bogomolov in conversation with Simon — Bogomolov (London) to Moscow, 5.2.32: *DVP SSSR*, vol. XV, doc. 68; the British record of this appears in Simon (London) to Ovey (Moscow), 5.2.32: *DBFP*, op. cit., doc. 151.

7. This was the work of Neville Chamberlain, now Chancellor of the Exchequer, imposing a 10% revenue tariff on all imports: *The Neville Chamberlain Papers, NC* 8/18/1.

8. Simon (London) to Ovey (Moscow), 5.2.32: *DBFP*, loc. cit., and Bogomolov (London) to Moscow, 5.2.32: *DVP SSSR*, loc. cit.

9. Chamberlain was, indeed, only too aware of Moscow's foreign exchange difficulties, justifying the curtailment of credit to British industrialists exporting to Russia by arguing that credit to Russia was "a gamble" because that country's financial position was "precarious" — Neville to Arthur Chamberlain, 11.2.32: *NC* 7/6/2.

10. For Bennett's statement, delivered on the 25 July: *Documents on Canadian External Relations*, Vol. 5, 1931–1935, edited by A.I.Inglis (Ottawa, 1973) doc. 63.

11. *DVP SSSR*, vol. XIV, doc. 117.

12. Reply to Bennett's statement, 25.7.32: *DCER*, op. cit., doc. 64.

13. Entry in Neville Chamberlain's diary, 18.8.32: *NC* /17.

14. *CAB* 51 (32).

15. Simon (London) to Ovey (Moscow), 17.10.32: *DBFP*, op. cit., doc. 165; and *DVP SSSR*, vol. XV, p. 674.

16. Ovey (Moscow) to Simon, 19.10.32: *DBFP*, op. cit., doc. 166; for Litvinov's record of the conversation: *DVP SSSR*, op. cit., doc. 411.

17. The Soviet record of the conversation on this subject early in October between Simon and Sokol'nikov has not been reproduced in full. But in an extract reprinted, Simon's reply to Sokol'nikov's question as to whether the British had contracted any obligation under the Ottawa agreement, was that "there is no such obligation": ibid., p. 799. Yet Simon's own record of the conversation gives a very brief summary and omits any such statement — Simon (London) to Strang (London), 6.10.32: *DBFP*, op. cit., doc. 163.

18. See note 15.

19. This is evident from the position on this issue taken by the Politburo: Krestinsky (Moscow) to Maisky (London), 3.11.32: *DVP SSSR*, op. cit., doc. 425.

20. Entry for 10.12.31: *Diary of Beatrice Webb*, vol. 44, p. 5222.
21. Entry for 7.3.32: ibid., p. 5283.
22. Beatrice Webb to Friends of Seaham, 23.7.23: *Letters of Sidney and Beatrice Webb*, vol. 3, *Pilgrimage 1912–1947*, edited by N. Mackenzie (Cambridge, 1978) p. 176.
23. Entry for 31.5.30: *Diary*, p. 4938.
24. Entry for 28.7.32: ibid., p. 5421.
25. *The New Statesman*, vol. IV, no. 94 (10.12.32), p. 770.
26. Entry for 4.2.31: *Diary*, p. 5066.
27. *Izvestiya*, 8.8.31.
28. Ivan Maisky, *Who Helped Hitler?* (London, 1964) p. 18.
29. Sperling (Helsinki) to London, 23.9.32: *FO* 371/16339.
30. Ovey (Moscow) to Simon (London), 20.10.32: ibid. The Webbs found him "a more accomplished diplomat and less ardent Communist" than his predecessor Sokol'nikov: *Diary*, p. 5375.

CHAPTER 11   FALSE OPTIMISM ON THE EVE OF HITLER'S VICTORY

1. The grave crisis in Soviet agriculture led directly to a questioning of Stalin's leadership and there were rumours that Stalin offered his resignation. The evidence on this is only circumstantial but comes from various sources, all of whom were in Moscow at the time: V. Serge, *Portrait de Staline* (Paris, 1940), p. 95; N. Basseches, *STALIN* (London, 1952); and Strang (Moscow) to Simon (London), 11.10.32: *FO* 371/16322. The resultant disciplinary measures taken by the regime against the embryonic opposition within the Party early in October may not have been as severe as Stalin would have liked, thus leaving him still in a state of insecurity. He was then hit by the death of his wife on the 8 November, an event which appears to have left him incapable of making clear decisions for a number of weeks. A report from the British embassy in Moscow dated the 12 December gives some indication of the paralysis now gripping the counsels of state:

> Affairs are now going so quickly from bad to worse that they dare not tell the truth to Stalin. Stalin, who, since his recent domestic tragedy, is reported to be more morose and silent than ever, is said to be living in a void no one dare enter with the truth on his lips.

   – Ovey (Moscow) to Simon (London), 12.12.32: *FO* 371/16324.
2. Editorial, "Novaya pobeda mirnoi politiki SSSR", *Pravda*, 28.11.32.
3. "Narastanie revolyutsionnogo pod"ema i zadachi kompartii Germanii", *Kommunisticheskii Internatsional*, No. 27, 30.9.32, pp. 81–95, and *Bol'shevik*, no. 21 (15.11.32) pp. 8–28.
4. "Does Hitler still exist?", asked Léon Bailby, in *L'Intransigeant* on the 29 September: cited in J-B. Duroselle, *La Décadence 1932–1939* (Paris, 1979) p. 58.
5. K. Egert, "Nachalo razlozheniya partii Gitlera", *Pravda*, 5.10.32.
6. Quoted by Duroselle, loc. cit.

7. Editorial, "Shest' millionov pod znamenem kommunizma", *Pravda*, 10.11.32.
8. Khinchuk (Berlin) to Krestinsky (Moscow), 20.11.32: *DVP SSSR*, vol. xv, doc. 444.
9. Litvinov's record of the conversation, 9.11.32: ibid., doc. 431.
10. For the Franco-Soviet pact: ibid., doc. 456.
11. See note 2.
12. G. Cioranesco et al., *Aspects des relations russo-roumaines* (Paris, 1967) pp. 128–9.
13. Editorial, "Sovetsko-frantsuzskii pakt o nenapadenii", *Pravda*, 30.11.32.
14. Under the influence of alcohol the Soviet chief of staff, Yegorov, told a British diplomat (evidently sober) as early as February 1932 that Russia sought an alliance with France, Romania and Poland – Ovey (Moscow) to Simon (London), 18.2.32: *FO* 371/16322.
15. Dejean (Moscow) to Paul-Boncour (Paris), 19.12.32: *DDF*, op. cit., doc. 122.
16. Krestinsky (Moscow) to Khinchuk (Berlin), 1.12.32: *DVP SSSR*, op. cit., doc. 466.
17. Krestinsky's record of the conversation, 3.12.32: ibid., p. 809.
18. Attolico (Moscow) to Rome, 23.8.32: *ASD*, URSS (1932), b. 6, f. 1.4.
19. Editorial, "Pravitel'stvo fon-Papena bez Papena", *Pravda*, 6.12.32.
20. Litvinov's record of the conversation *DVP SSSR*, op. cit., doc. 487 – carefully omits these controversial comments; for the German record, however, see *AA* 1417/2860, 562400–2.
21. See Appendix 2.
22. For the exchange of notes: *DVP SSSR*, op. cit., doc. 480. It was announced by Litvinov in an interview with the press: ibid., doc. 481; see also, editorial, "Vosstanovlenie sovetsko-kitaiskikh diplomaticheskikh otnoshenii", *Pravda*, 13.12.32.
23. Litvinov (Geneva) to Moscow, 13.12.32: *DVP SSSR*, op. cit., doc. 482.
24. Reported by TASS, 13.12.32: ibid., p. 814.
25. The Japanese note is reprinted in *DVP SSSR*, vol. xvi, doc. 2 (enclosure).

12 CONCLUSION

1. Attolico (Moscow) to Rome, 31.5.32: *ASD*, B.5, URSS (1932), f.1.1.
2. Memorandum by Mr Paton – enclosed in Ovey (Moscow) to Simon (London), 19.12.32: *DBFP*, Second Series, vol. vii, doc. 201.

APPENDIX 1

1. Anton Ciliga, *The Russian Enigma* (1940, reprinted Connecticut, 1973) p. 95.
2. *FO* 371/14887.
3. Ovey (Moscow) to Henderson (London) 28.3.30: *DBFP*, vol. vii, doc. 77.
4. *AD*, URSS, 925.
5. Cerruti (Moscow) to Rome, 22.3.30: *ASD*, 1559, Russia (1930).

6. Cerruti (Moscow) to Rome, 10.4.30: ibid.

APPENDIX 2

1. See pp. 53–4.
2. *Vneshnyaya Torgovlya SSSR v Gody Dovoennykh Pyatiletok (1929–1940): Statisticheskii Sbornik* (Moscow, 1968).
3. *New York Times*, 5.1.32.
4. Ibid., 22.4.32.
5. Skvirsky (Washington) to Moscow, 2.12.32: *DVP SSSR*, vol. xv, doc. 468.
6. Skvirsky (Washington) to Moscow, 10.1.33: quoted in ibid., pp. 809–10.

A Bibliographical Note

The sources listed below have clearly not all been of equal value, though it is impossible to single out any one item as being of supreme importance. The most that can be done is to point to those which have proved the more useful.

Without the volumes of diplomatic correspondence edited in Moscow, a work of this nature would still have been possible to construct, but it would have lacked the kind of definition required. It would, for example, have made it that more difficult to penetrate the curtain of words in the Soviet press and official pronouncements which form the customary source material for analyses of Soviet foreign policy, past and present. It is also apparent that these volumes have been edited according to criteria as to that which throws better light on the Soviet regime's actions and intentions. Happily these criteria vary from volume to volume along with changing editors, though on the whole potentially embarrassing documents are carefully omitted.

This means that other diplomatic archives can render a useful service. It is far easier to keep one's domestic rather than diplomatic secrets, for the simple reason that all international relations are at minimum bilateral, and rapid alterations in alliances and alignments facilitate the release of material compromising other Powers. All other major European states have now opened their diplomatic archives for the 1930s. Clearly not all the documents are available for consultation. Some perished in the war; others are simply locked away. But taken together the British, French, Italian and German archives represent an invaluable means of uncovering those dimensions to Soviet foreign policy which Moscow prefers to leave cloaked in secrecy.

A further major source are Soviet periodicals. Moscow's diplomatic correspondence as published reflects only one part of Soviet thinking. Party opinions, in particular, are not well represented. For these one has to turn to the Soviet press which, when correctly interpreted, often conveys a sense of atmosphere

157

that is missing from diplomatic telegrams, as well as a strength of feeling considered inappropriate to diplomatic usage. Similarly Soviet memoirs – unfortunately all too rare – and anecdotes related in secondary sources published in the USSR often add a touch of colour.

As to secondary sources in Russian the late A.E. Ioffe's work covers Soviet foreign policy from 1928 to 1932. Edited under Maisky's supervision, it represents a thorough and comprehensive review of Soviet foreign relations where economic matters are concerned, but simultaneously sidesteps most of the more awkward political issues confronting Moscow at the time. In English Max Beloff's history, although formally dating from 1929, in effect only begins substantially in 1933 and has therefore, and for no other reason, been omitted from the list below. The late E.H.Carr's forthcoming history of the Comintern during this period, which I have seen prior to publication, will undoubtedly fill in a much needed gap in our knowledge of Soviet policy at this time. Of a more specialist nature, two other monographs must be mentioned: the late Thomas Weingartner's exhaustive study of the Comintern and Germany, and Scott's impressively meticulous analysis of Franco-Soviet relations leading up to 1935.

Bibliography

A: PRIMARY SOURCES

I: Unpublished

(a) Britain: *Cabinet Minutes* (Public Record Office, London).
Committee of Imperial Defence: Minutes (PRO).
Diary of Beatrice Webb (British Library of Political and Economic Science, London).
Foreign Office: Diplomatic Correspondence (PRO).
The Neville Chamberlain Papers (Birmingham University Library).
(b) France: *Diplomatic Correspondence* (Quai d'Orsay, Paris).
National Archives (Overseas Section, rue Oudinot, Paris).
(c) Germany: *Diplomatic Correspondence* (Photostats, FCO Records, London).
(d) Italy: *Diplomatic Correspondence* (Farnesina, Rome).
Political Police Archives (Central State Archives, Rome).

II: Published

(a) USSR and Comintern

Annuaire Diplomatique du Commissariat du Peuple pour les Affaires Etrangères. 1934 (Moscow, 1935?).
Vneshnyaya Torgovlya SSSR v Gody Dovoennykh Pyatiletok (1929–1940): Statisticheskii Sbornik (Moscow, 1968).
XII Plenum IKKI: Stenograficheskii Otchet (Moscow, 1933).
Dokumenty Vneshnei Politiki SSSR, Vols:
  VII, edited by G.K.Deev et al. (Moscow, 1963).
  X, ed. I.M.Gorokhov et al. (Moscow, 1965).
  XII, ed. I.I.Agayants et al. (Moscow, 1967).
  XIII, ed. G.K.Deev et al. (Moscow, 1967).
  XIV, ed. P.I.Yershov et al. (Moscow, 1968).
  XV, ibid. (Moscow, 1969).
  XVI, ed. F.P.Dolya et al. (Moscow, 1970).
Iz Istorii Mezhdunarodnoi Proletarskoi Solidarnosti: Dokumenty i Materialy, Sbornik IV: Mezhdunarodnaya Proletarskaya Solidarnost' v Bor'be s Nastupleniem Fashizma (1928–1932), ed. G.A.Belov et al. (Moscow, 1960).
Lenin, V.I., *Collected Works*, vol. 42 (Moscow, 1969) and vol. 45 (Moscow, 1970).
Mezhdunarodnye Otnosheniya 1870–1918 gg: Sbornik Dokumentov, ed. V.M.Khvostov (Moscow, 1940).
XI Plenum IKKI: Stenograficheskii Otchet. Vypusk II (Moscow–Leningrad, 1931).

159

Le Parti communiste français devant l'Internationale (Paris, 1931).
Pogranichnye Voiska SSSR 1918–1928: Sbornik Dokumentov ed. P.I.Zyryanov et al. (Moscow, 1973).
Ibid., *1929–1938*, ibid. (Moscow, 1972).
50 Let Bor'by SSSR za Razoruzhenie: Sbornik Dokumentov ed. K.V. Novikov *et al.* (Moscow, 1967).
XVII S"ezd Vsesoyuznoi Kommunisticheskoi Partii (B): Stenograficheskii Otchet (Moscow, 1934).
Stalin, J.V., *Works*, vol. 13 (Moscow, 1955).
XVI S"ezd Vsesoyuznoi Kommunisticheskoi Partii (B): Stenograficheskii Otchet (Moscow, 1931).
United Front Against War: Report and Manifesto of the World Anti-War Congress at Amsterdam (London, 1932).

(b) Other Countries
AKTEN DER REICHSKANZLEI: Weimarer Republik: Das Kabinett Müller, 28. Juni 1928 bis 27. März 1930: Band 2: August 1929 bis März 1930, ed. M.Vogt (Boppard am Rhein, 1970).
I Documenti Diplomatici Italiani, 7 Serie: 1922–1935, vol. IX, ed. R.Moscati et al. (Rome, 1975).
Documents on British Foreign Policy 1919–1939, 2nd Series, vol. I, ed. E.L.Woodward and R. Butler (London, 1946).
II, ibid. (London, 1947).
III, ibid. (London. 1948).
VII, ibid., (London, 1958).
Documents on Canadian External Relations, vol. 5, ed. A.Inglish (Ottawa, 1973).
Documents Diplomatiques Français 1932–1939, 1st series, Vol. I, ed. M.Baumont, P. Renouvin et al. (Paris, 1964) Vol. IV, ibid. (Paris, 1968).
Documents on International Affairs 1931, ed. J.Wheeler-Bennett (London, 1932).
Documents on International Affairs 1932, ed. J.Wheeler-Bennett (London, 1933).
Foreign Relations of the United States: The Soviet Union 1933–1939 (Washington, 1952).
Journal Officiel: Chambre de Députés.
Judgement: International Military Tribunal for the Far East.
Letters of Sidney and Beatrice Webb, vol. 3, *Pilgrimage 1912–1947*, ed N.Mackenzie (Cambridge, 1978).
Parliamentary Debates: the House of Commons.
71st Congress, 3rd Session, House of Representatives, report No. 2290 INVESTIGATION OF COMMUNIST PROPAGANDA

Periodicals

Bol'shevik
The Daily Express
The Daily Worker
The Economist
Ekonomicheskaya Zhizn'

Moscow Daily News
Moskauer Rundschau
Na Agrarnom Fronte
New Statesman
New York Times

Esprit
l'Europe Nouvelle
Gazeta Warszawska
l'Humanité
Izvestiya
Kommunisticheskii Internatsional
Krasnaya Zvezda
Leningradskaya Pravda
Le Matin
Mezhdunarodnaya Letopis'
Mezhdunarodnaya Zhizn'
Mirovoe Khozyaistvo i Mirovaya Politika

Novyi Vostok
Posev
Pravda
Revolyutsionny Vostok

Spravochnik Partiinogo Rabotnika
Le Temps
The Times
Vie Économique des Soviets
Voenno-Istoricheskii Zhurnal
Voennyi Vestnik
Za Industrializatsiyu

B: REFERENCE WORKS

Biographical Dictionary of the Comintern, ed. B. Lazitch and M.M.
   Drachkovich (Stanford, 1973).
Bol'shaya Sovetskaya Entsiklopediya (third edition), vol. 13, ed. A. Prokhorov et
   al. (Moscow, 1973).
Diplomaticheskii Slovar', vol. 3, ed. A.F.Miller et al. (Moscow, 1973).
Who Was Who in the USSR, ed. H.F.Schulz et al. (New Jersey, USA, 1972).

C: MEMOIRS AND KINDRED WORKS

Barmine, A., One Who Survived (New York, 1945).
Basseches, N., STALIN (London, 1951).
Bérard, A., Un ambassadeur se souvient: au temps du danger allemand
   (Paris, 1976).
Besedovsky, G.Z., Na Putyakh k Termidoru (Paris, 1930).
Braun, O., Kitaiskie Zapiski (Moscow, 1974).
Ciliga, A., The Russian Enigma (reprint, Connecticut, USA, 1973).
Duranty, W., STALIN AND CO: The Politburo – The Men Who Run Russia
   (London, 1949).
Fischer, L., Men and Politics: An Autobiography (New York, 1941).
François-Poncet, A., The Fateful Years: Memoirs of a French Ambassador in
   Berlin 1931–1938 (New York, 1949).
Hart, L., The Memoirs of Captain Liddell Hart, vol. 1 (London, 1965).
Herbette, J., Ein französischer Diplomat über die bolschewistische Gefahr.
   Berichte des Botschafters der französischen Republik in Moskau in den Jahren
   1927–1931 (Berlin, 1943).
Herriot, E., Jadis: d'une guerre à l'autre 1914–1936 (Paris, 1952).
Litvinov, I., She Knew She Was Right (London, 1971).
Maisky, I., Lyudi, Sobytiya, Fakty (Moscow, 1973).
_____, Vospominaniya Sovetskogo Diplomata (Moscow, 1971).
_____, Who Helped Hitler? (London, 1964).
Papen, F., von Memoirs (London, 1952).
Roy, M.N., Men I Met (Bombay, 1968).

Serge, V., *Mémoires d'un révolutionnaire 1901–1941* (Paris, 1951).
———, *Portrait de Staline* (Paris, 1940).
Voitsekhovsky, S.L., *TREST: Vospominaniya i Dokumenty* (Canada, 1974).
Vospominaniya o Georgii Dimitrove (Sofia, 1972).
"Yoshizawa gaisō no Nisso fukashin jōyaku, Manshū jihen ni kansuru kaisōdan", *Kokusai Seiji*, no. 1 (1966).

D: SECONDARY WORKS

Avtorkhanov, A., *Proiskhozhdenie partokratii, 2: TsK i Stalin* (Frankfurt am Main, 1973).
Bariéty, J. and Bloch, C., "Une tentative de réconciliation franco-allemande et son échec (1932–1933)", *Revue d'Histoire Moderne et Contemporaine*, vol. xv, July–September 1968.
Beckermann, G., and Genji, O., *The Japanese Communist Party 1922–1945* (Stanford, 1969).
Carr, E.H., *The Bolshevik Revolution 1917–1923*, vol. 3 (London, 1953).
———, *The Interregnum 1923–1924* (London, 1960).
———, *Socialism in One Country 1924–1926*, vol. 3 (London, 1964).
———, *Foundations of a Planned Economy 1926–1929* (London, 1976–8).
Cioranescu, G., *et al.*, *Aspects des relations Russo-Roumaines* (Paris, 1967).
Cooper, J., "Defence Production and the Soviet Economy 1929–1941", *CREES Discussion Papers*, Series SIPS, no. 3 (Brimingham, 1976).
Davies, R.W., *The Industrialisation of Soviet Russia, 1: The Socialist Offensive – The Collectivisation of Soviet Agriculture 1929–1930* (London, 1980).
Georgii Dimitrov: an Outstanding Militant of the Comintern (English edition, Sofia, 1972).
Duroselle, J-B., *La Décadence 1932–1939* (Paris, 1979).
Dushen'kin, V., *Proletarskii Marshal* (Moscow, 1973).
Dyck, H.L., *Weimar Germany and Soviet Russia 1926–1933: A Study in Diplomatic Instability* (London, 1966).
Eyck, E., *A History of the Weimar Republic* (New York, 1970).
Felice, R. de, *Mussolini il duce: I, Gli anni del consenso 1929–1936* (Turin, 1974).
Fischer, L., *Russia's Road From Peace to War: Soviet Foreign Relations 1917–1941* (New York, 1969).
Flechtheim, O.K., *Die KPD in der Weimarer Republik* (Frankfurt am Main, 1969).
Geschichte der deutschen Arbeiterbewegung, vol. 4 (Berlin, 1966).
Grey, M., *Le Général meurt à Minuit: l'enlèvement de Koutiepov 1930 et de Miller 1937* (Paris, 1981).
Gross, B., *WILLI MÜNZENBERG: Eine politische Biographie* (Stuttgart, 1967).
Ioffe, A.E., *Vneshnyaya Politika Sovetskogo Soyuza 1928–1932 gg* (Moscow, 1968).
Kitsikis, D., "La Grèce et le projet Briand d'Union européenne du 1er mai 1930", *Revue d'Histoire Moderne et Contemporaine*, vol. xii, 1965.

Kobolev, E.B., "Ho Chi Minh – Velikii Syn V'etnama", *Novaya i Noveishaya Istoriya*, no. 5 (1976).

Krutitskaya, E.I., and Mitrofanova, S., *Polpred Aleksandr Troyanovsky* (Moscow, 1975).

Kuo, W., *Analytical History of the Chinese Communist Party* (2nd edn, Taipei, 1968).

Kutakov, L.N., *Istoriya Sovetsko-Yaponskikh Diplomaticheskikh Otnoshenii* (Moscow, 1962).

Mikhutina, I.V., *Sovetsko-Pol'skie Otnosheniya 1931–1935* (Moscow, 1977).

Nove, A., *An Economic History of the USSR* (Penguin edition, London, 1972).

Ogata, S., *Defiance in Manchuria* (Berkeley, 1964).

Pelling, H., *The British Communist Party: A Historical Profile* (London, 1958).

Récits de la résistance vietnamienne (1925–1945) (Paris, 1964).

Scott, W.E., *Alliance Against Hitler: The Origins of the Franco-Soviet Pact* (London, 1962).

Shiltova, A.P., and Mordvinov, V.F., *Natsional'no-Osvoboditel'noe Dvizhenie vo V'etname (1858–1945)* (Moscow, 1958).

Shirinya, K.K., *Strategiya i Taktika Kominterna v Bor'be Protiv Fashizma i Voiny (1934–1939 gg)* (Moscow, 1979).

Spriano, P., *Storia del Partito comunista italiano: II, Gli anni della clandestinità* (Turin, 1969).

Suarez, G., *BRIAND: sa vie – son oeuvre, VI, 1923–1932* (Paris, 1952).

Sykes, C., *NANCY: The Life of Lady Astor* (London, 1972).

Thorne, C., *The Limits of Foreign Policy: The West, the League and the Far Eastern Crisis of 1931–1933* (London, 1972).

Ullman, R.H., *ANGLO-SOVIET RELATIONS 1917–1921*, Vol. 1: *Intervention and the War* (London, 1961).

Vidnye Sovetskie Kommunisty – Uchastniki Kitaiskoi Revolyutsii (Moscow, 1970).

Weingartner, T., *Stalin und der Aufstieg Hitlers. Die Deutschlandpolitik die Sowjetunion und die Kommunistische Internationale 1929–1934* (Berlin, 1970).

Yanguzov, Z.Sh., *Osobaya Krasnoznamennaya Dal'nevostochnaya Armiya na Strazhe Mira i Bezopasnosti SSSR (1929–1938 gg)* (Blagoveshchensk, 1970).

Zakharov, et al., *Tikhookeanskii Flot* (Moscow, 1966).

Zarnowski, J., (ed.), *PRZYJAŹNIE I ANTAGONIZMY: Stosunki Polski z Państwami Sąsiednimi w Latach 1918–1939* (Warsaw, 1977).

Zhukovsky, N., *Na Diplomaticheskom Postu* (Moscow, 1973).

Index